Shatto Arthur Gakwandi has accomplished two major tasks in this book. Firstly he provides an excellent critical assessment of twelve major novels from Africa. Secondly, through this assessment, he outlines the main concerns of African fiction.

In particular he is concerned with the parallel relationship between nationalism and modern African literature. His discussion strikes an admirable balance between the evaluation of the literary merits of the novel and the interpretation of the novel as a social document.

He maintains that 'the African novel has developed as a response to the far-reaching social revolution of the twentieth century on the continent'. This persistent view gives the book a thematic unity which means that, read as a whole, the essays on the chosen pairs of novels reinforce a central and significant argument.

The Novel and Contemporary Experience in Africa

The Novel and Contemporary Experience in Africa

SHATTO ARTHUR GAKWANDI

Senior Lecturer in Literature
Makerere University, Kampala

AFRICANA PUBLISHING COMPANY
NEW YORK

First published in the United States of America 1977 by
Africana Publishing Company
a division of
Holmes & Meier Publishers, Inc.
101 Fifth Avenue
New York, New York 10003

Library of Congress Cataloging in Publication Data
Gakwandi, Shatto Arthur.
The novel and contemporary experience in Africa.

1. African fiction (English)—History and criticism.
I. Title.
PR9344.G3 823'.03 77-1273
ISBN 0-8419-0306-9

PRINTED IN GREAT BRITAIN

Contents

Acknowledgements

The author and publisher would like to thank the following for permission to reproduce copyright material:

André Deutsch for extracts from *The Gab Boys* by Cameron Duodu, 1967.

Elaine Green for world rights on the extracts from *The Gab Boys* © Cameron Duodu, 1967.

Heinemann Educational Books for extracts from *The Beautyful Ones Are Not Yet Born* by Ayi Kwei Armah, African Writers Series, 1969.

Houghton Mifflin Company for American rights on *The Beautyful Ones Are Not Yet Born* by Ayi Kwei Armah, 1968.

John Farquharson Ltd for extracts from *A Wreath for Udomo* by Peter Abrahams published by Faber and Faber, 1956.

Publisher's Note

When two dates are given for the publication of a book, the date in brackets refers to when the book was first published. The other date is the publication date of the African Writers Series edition, published by Heinemann Educational Books.

Introduction: Historical and Literary Background

ALL twentieth century intellectual movements in Africa have been, in one way or another, associated with nationalism. Nationalism and modern African literature have followed closely parallel courses and derived reciprocal inspiration one from the other, both being part of an awakening and a search for a new place in the world for the African. While written literature was already appearing on the continent as early as the beginning of the century and the roots of this literature can be traced back to Afro-American writings of the eighteenth and nineteenth centuries, a tradition with its own distinctive characteristics did not begin to emerge until the early fifties. Over the last two decades of its growth African literature has been dominated by one major theme, an assessment of Africa's contact with the West. The spiritual and social implications of this contact have been the concern of most writers. Characteristically, the meeting of Africa and Europe has been presented as a conflict. The lesser writers have been content with a general presentation of typical incompatibilities, but the better writers have dug deeper and attempted to determine the specific implications of this conflict for particular African communities.

The attainment of independence by many African countries in the early sixties brought about a noticeable decline in the theme of cultural conflict, until in the most recent works one is hardly aware of warring or opposed ways of life. But the contradictions of modern Africa which stem from the co-existence of widely differing values are still the inescapable reality which the writer has to deal with. As Aimé Césaire once said:

> Whether we like it or not, we cannot pose the problem of native cultures without at the same time posing the problem of colonialism, for all native cultures are today developing under the peculiar influence of a colonial, semi-colonial or para-colonial situation.[1]

Modern African literature has been largely concerned with interpreting the more recent implications of a history extending over the last four centuries. It may be useful therefore to say a few words about significant features of this history which have attracted the creative imagination. Africa's contact with the West began towards the end of the fifteenth century when the Portuguese explorer, Vasco da Gama, called into a few harbours along the West African coast. But the slave trade, which started on a large scale about a century later, was the first great phenomenon which shook Africa out of centuries of quietude and isolation and began a long period of wars and conflicts which were to last until artificial stability was imposed by the European powers when they decided to divide and rule the continent directly. During the period of slave-trade the West must have remained a cruel mystery to most Africans; the social turbulence would have been too vast and too hard to comprehend. This, together with the wide-spread illiteracy which existed on the continent must be part of the explanation for the long delay in the emergence of written literature. Not surprisingly, therefore, it was amongst the group of Africans who crossed the seas and came into closer contact with the West that the first seeds of the new literature were sown. Their experience had brought to them a greater understanding of the process of history in which they were caught than could be attained by the African in his native place. Several ex-slaves wrote accounts of their experiences to expose the cruelties of Western civilization, one of the best known of these accounts being by Olaudah Equiano.[2] In this account we can recognize the ambivalence of the African who has suffered the injustices of the West but is in that very process set apart from the simpler values of his original community. Poets such as Phillis Wheatly and George Moses Horton deplored their enslaved condition but were prepared to embrace the values of Western civilization in which they had been initiated. This eighteenth and nineteenth century literature by black people in the new world has been referred to by Janheinz Jahn as 'apprentice literature'[3] because it generally tried to imitate European models of the period. However, within it, we see the beginnings of protest against the injustice of the white races and the growth of ambivalent attitudes towards these races, both of which have been the subject of much modern black writing.

African nationalism and pan-Africanism started in the new world and the leaders of these movements on the African continent were deeply influenced by thinkers such as Dr William DuBois and Marcus Garvey. Indeed Colin Legum[4] sees DuBois as the first major link between political consciousness and literary awakening. The six conferences on pan-Africanism which the two leaders organized in various European capitals (including one in New York) between 1900 and 1945 were to play a decisive role in the growth of nationalism among African students who were studying abroad. It was at the sixth pan-African congress in Manchester in 1945 that political independence was first proclaimed as a goal of nationalism. The previous congresses had been concerned with social and legal equality for the colonial peoples. Meanwhile the contact between the West Indian and African intellectuals in Paris led to the growth of a new literary movement which in the forties became known as negritude. This movement was mainly concerned with a rediscovery of salutary elements in the African traditional way of life. In many ways the nineteenth century Afro-American romantic essayist, Edward Blyden, was the precursor of this movement. Blyden was the first black man to attempt an objective appraisal of African cultures. In an essay 'Africa's Service to the World'[5] he traced the history of Africa's contact with the outside world and produced evidence from sociology, history, and literature to show that Africa had something positive to offer the world. His writings are coloured by the romantic views of his contemporary world. When he writes: 'In visions of the future, I behold those beautiful hills—the banks of those charming streams ... in primaeval innocence', one sees how close he is to the post-Wordsworthian tradition. But Blyden reached beyond romanticism and tried to rehabilitate the living cultures of African communities which had been abused by three centuries of degradation. He took pride in his blackness and implored his fellow Afro-Americans to do the same. He urged the black races to embrace their history and their culture and use them as the foundation for building the future. Modern scholarship, which has attempted to rehabilitate African culture and to view African history in a more scientific perspective, must acknowledge a debt to Blyden.

Here, however, we are concerned with the novel, and it is the development of this form that we shall now trace. The novel is the predominant creative form in Africa today, but although it has overtaken the essay, poetry and drama, it is relatively new on the African literary scene. The beginnings of the modern African novel might be traced to Mofolo's *Chaka*,[6] a historical romance which was written in Sesotho early in this century. According to Janheinz Jahn this book was written in 1908 but its publication was delayed by the author's missionary patrons because of 'pagan' elements in it which were considered to be anti-Christian and it was not published until 1925. Solomon Plaatje's *Mhudi*[7] appeared in 1930. Scattered minor works began to appear mainly in South, but also in East and Central, Africa. However, the first non-white African novelist to gain a wide reading public was Peter Abrahams whose first novel, *Song of the City*,[8] appeared in 1945. But it was not until the fifties that the African novel began to acquire its own identity and generate the present literary explosion.

So the 'tradition' of African fiction with which we are dealing here spans barely two decades. This naturally raises certain problems. To talk of

English literature, Russian literature or French literature is to assume a tradition in which writers grow up, which influences them before they contribute to it. Every writer is influenced by the tradition in which he acquires his tools of writing: the language, the styles and the forms which he is familiar with before he starts writing. The modern African writer acquires his tools through contact with at least one of the Western literatures. According to a study made by Lilyan Kesteloot[9] most African writers of French expression have been influenced by French, Russian and American literatures in that order. Many of the writers who were interviewed claimed to have been influenced by vernacular literatures of their communities. Since no comprehensive study of the numerous vernacular litaratures of the continent has yet been made it is difficult to assess the degree to which they have influenced writers. Yet to talk of the African novel is to assume that it has its own distinctive characteristics which distinguish it from novels from other areas of the world written in the same language.

Critics such as Janheinz Jahn[10] have defended the view that there is an essential similarity between all literatures written by people whose origins can be traced back to Africa. This rather tenuous assumption has been adopted by Claude Wauthier.[11] To give this assumption any credibility evidence would be needed to show that there was cultural coherence in Africa before its contact with the West; but since no such evidence has yet been produced by sociologists and historians it seems more reasonable to accept the view that the common elements of modern African culture stem from patterns imposed by colonialism. As Le Vine has stated:

> There is no lack of documentation for the proposition that the colonial period in Africa produced several trans-territorial political cultures that survived the transition to independence and that continue to affect the internal and external politics of the post-colonial African states. These trans-territorial cultures are modern rather than traditional in the sense that their participants are mainly the products of the westernized strata of African society. They are élite political cultures involving only a small proportion of Africans, most of whom occupy positions of influence, and excluding the politically unsophisticated African masses. These élite cultures rest upon shared political values, common or similar political experiences, common educational backgrounds, shared nationalist symbols.[12]

This peculiar development of trans-national cultures is the basis on which we shall attempt to identify and discuss certain thematic as well as stylistic features of modern African literature. It is on this basis that John Povey has asserted that 'there is justification for declaring that African literature in

English is a separate and new area which may be considered in relation to contemporary Africa, and without reference to vernacular writing.'[13]

Because nationalist sentiments have dominated the ideological aspirations of African peoples in this century certain common values have been shared by writers from Africa during this period. Before the growth of nationalism it was much more difficult for an African writer to choose a standpoint from which to interpret his experience. The nationalist stance has provided a facility for the modern African writer to assess and comment upon his contemporary experience.

From its beginnings African nationalism tried to use literature as an instrument of political liberation. Conferences of Negro writers sprang up as offshoots of the pan-African congresses which tried to direct all intellectual activity in the service of nationalist causes. The first Congress of Negro Writers was held in Paris in 1956. Since that time numerous conferences have been held and many of them have tried to exhort African authors to identify with the social needs of the continent, and to advance the cause of nationalism. At this first congress in 1956 one of the delegates, Emmanuel C. Paul, declared:

> To contribute to the revision of the whole series of representations upon which colonialism relies to justify itself, that seems to us, at the moment, to be the most urgent task of the Negro writer. . . .[14]

Another delegate, Ben Enwonwu, insisted in an even more impassioned declaration on the need for literature to put itself at the service of nationalism:

> The present generation of African artists therefore have to face their political problems, and try to look at art through politics; the kind of picture that the political aspect of African art shows is one of strife and pity.[15]

Many of these congresses which were organized under the auspices of *Présence Africaine* ended by passing long lists of resolutions laying down principles which were to guide Negro writers. At the Second Congress of Negro Artists and Writers in Rome in 1959 a general resolution recommended, among other things, that:

> The negro writers and artists regard it as their essential task and sacred mission to bring their cultural activity within the scope of the great movement for liberation of their individual peoples, without losing sight of the solidarity which should unite all individuals and peoples who are struggling for the liquidation of colonization and its consequences as well as all those who are fighting throughout the world for progress and liberty.[16]

The pattern of thinking has changed a great deal since that time and more recent conferences of African writers have avoided passing prescriptive resolutions. In particular, the idea that the philosophy of negritude should be the nurse of all African writing has been rejected by writers from the English-speaking area.

Even within the French-speaking area negritude is increasingly being discredited. African thinkers are beginning to accept that there are wide differences within their traditional cultures and that the notion of an African essence is an illusion. It is becoming widely accepted that the broad similarities of the African experience from which writers draw their creative material is modern rather than ancient and that it stems from the shared history which is fairly recent. The first Pan-African Festival in 1969 which was by far the most wide-ranging gathering of its kind ever to be held in Africa, reflected views which show that an increasing number of writers no longer accepts a simple ideology as a basis for all Africa's creative efforts. In a penetrating analysis of the present trends in African culture, Dahomey's Commissioner General for Culture and Youth, Stanislav Adotevi, declared:

> In concrete terms it will no longer do to talk of African unity; we must pursue the means. We can no longer content ourselves with abstract affirmations about African culture in general; we must elucidate scientifically what it is that makes such and such a manifestation distinctly African Negro, another Maghrabin and a third by origin and inspiration strictly Arab. This is the truth, eroded sometimes by the passage of time but confirmed by circumstance. All of us share the desire to bridge centuries and differences and to create a united present.[17]

The *Pan-African Cultural Manifesto* which was formulated by the symposium reflects an acceptance of the view that many of the links of present-day African cultures arise directly from a sense of common destiny which has come about as a result of the colonial experience. Part of the *Manifesto* reads:

> Beyond similarities and convergent forms of thought, beyond the common heritage, Africanity is also a shared destiny, the fraternity of the liberation struggle and a common future which should be assumed by all in order to master it. Africanity springs from the double source of our common heritage and our common destiny and that is why it is worthwhile, at the present stage of our historical development, to examine a number of problems linked with the origin, the existence and the development of our culture.[18]

Although most of the countries which participated are politically independent there is a preoccupation with voicing anti-colonial sentiments.

Nationalism is still the main driving force behind the political and cultural trends in modern Africa. This is the prevalent consciousness, the intellectual milieu within which artists create. Negritude may be losing ground but there is a continual search for another political standpoint from which African intellectuals will be able to interpret their experience. Evident in the *Manifesto*, however, and reflected in many recent writings, is an attempt to look towards the future rather than to the past. The sense of a shared destiny is as important as the sense of a shared past. The *Manifesto* declares:

> Culture is essentially dynamic: in other words it is both rooted in the people and oriented towards the future. We must go back to the sources of our values, not to confine ourselves to them, but rather to draw up a critical inventory in order to get rid of archaic stultifying elements, the fallacious and alienating foreign elements brought in by colonialism, and to retain only those elements which are still valid, bringing them up to date and enriching them with the benefits of the scientific, technical and social revolutions so as to bring them into line with what is modern and universal.[19]

There is no suggestion here that all these resolutions and manifestos passed at various conferences reflect the attitudes of individual writers. What they do reflect is the way in which nationalist sentiments and the struggle for political freedom have been at the heart of most of Africa's creative activities. Indeed political concern is a characteristic feature of African literature. The demand for freedom, social justice and equality runs through African literature before and after independence.

As African literature grows it begins to acquire distinct characteristics in different parts of the continent. Already it is possible to talk of Nigerian literature and Margaret Laurence's critical study, *Long Drums and Cannons*[20] has assumed the existence of distinctive coherence within Nigerian literature. Most critics, however, have found it most convenient to divide African literature into three broad 'traditions': South African, Anglophone African and Francophone African. In South Africa the main emphasis has been on the evils of racialism; in French-speaking Africa the emphasis has been on asserting African identity and rejecting assimilation, while in English-speaking Africa the primary concern has been with portraying tensions which arise from the co-existence of two distinct ways of life, the Western and the traditional. This variation of emphasis in treating the same basic problem is a direct result of the different experiences of colonialism and white domination which the three separate areas have experienced.

The rather limited term 'protest literature' has often been applied to

African literature in general but the serious artists have always been concerned with more than gestures of protest. In South Africa on the other hand there is an understandable preoccupation among non-white writers with the evils of repression, police brutality and arbitrary imprisonment which has sometimes led to the kind of 'protest' literature which Ezekiel Mphahlele has often complained about.[21] At the beginning of the century South African writers in Bantu languages were recreating their past[22] in the same way as writers from other parts of the continent have been doing more recently—exploring their own history as a means of self-affirmation. Later writers such as Peter Abrahams and Ezekiel Mphahlele tend to be less preoccupied with the past and are more concerned with the present. The present in South Africa means *apartheid* and this is bound to be a major preoccupation of literature for both white and black writers from the republic. Alan Paton is very close to the early works of Peter Abrahams and Lewis Nkosi in portraying this denial of natural human relationships. All three expose the unnaturalness of the values imposed by apartheid and insist, often sentimentally, that love is bound to triumph in the end. Personal love is seen as a gesture which has an exemplary effect upon the community. However, as the South African situation changes from bad to worse, simple treatments of the old theme of love and human brotherhood begin to appear more and more inadequate and irrelevant. Another group of writers is distinguished by a calculated rejection of explicit protest. They portray the situation sensitively and let it speak for itself. Dan Jacobson, Nadine Gordimer and Ezekiel Mphahlele belong to this group. Some recent writers adopt an attitude closer to that of pure protest. Richard Rive and Alex La Guma belong to this group. But while Alex La Guma portrays nothing but hostility between the world of the white man and that of the black man, in his avoidance of explicit commentary he resembles the previous group. *A Walk in the Night*[23] is perhaps the most poignant distillation of this hostility. Here the black man's suffering and the white man's fears collide with irreconcilable ferocity. All other sentiments are subordinated to this collision. The total lack of communication between the two worlds is brought out however, less by statement than by external description, as in this, of two policemen walking towards the coloured protagonist of the novel:

> Michael Adonis turned towards the pub and saw the two policemen coming towards him. They came down the pavement in their flat caps, khaki shirts and pants, their gun harness shiny with polish, and the holstered pistols heavy at their waists. They had hard, frozen faces as if carved out of pink ice, and hard, dispassionate eyes, hard and bright as pieces of blue glass. They strolled slowly and determinedly side by side,

without moving off their course, cutting a path through the stream on the pavement like destroyers at sea. (pp. 10–11)

The metallic hardness of the policemen's movements, dress and appearance conveys their brute force and ruthlessness while the images of coldness—'frozen faces', 'pink ice'—make them out to be mechanical instruments of oppression. The policemen are a stark symbol of terror from which, wherever Adonis goes, he cannot escape. As Michael Adonis who has recently lost his job walks aimlessly around the streets of Cape Town he is constantly menaced by this ubiquitous symbol of terror.

Some novelists from Francophone Africa have expressed sharply their bitterness against colonialism. But their bitterness is usually qualified by a sense of humour. The hard-hitting satire of Mongo Beti and Ferdinand Oyono is double-edged: it uncovers the inhumanity which is inherent in colonialism while at the same time it exposes the folly of those who willingly submit to it. The two novelists usually portray heroes who are discovering painfully the inadequacy of the foreign values which they have naively accepted.

Other novelists from French-speaking Africa have treated variations of the same themes which have been written about by their counterparts writing in English. Cheikh Hamidou Kane's *L'Aventure Ambigue*,[24] for example, explores the same problems of a cultural clash which have been the preoccupation of African novelists writing in English. Kane's novel dwells much more on the spiritual plane while most other novels of the same school have attempted a search for social and political goals. While Kane's writing resembles Achebe's, that of Ousmane Sembene could be better related to that of James Ngugi, both portraying African communities in organized revolt against colonial exploitation.

Novel writing in English-speaking Africa, other than South Africa, is principally a post-independence phenomenon, which may help to explain the degree to which the protest element is subdued. The earliest novelists to make their mark on the public were Cyprian Ekwensi and Chinua Achebe, both from Nigeria. They started writing in the fifties when independence was already in view. In such a situation it was possible to look back with comparative dispassion, over the history of colonialism and try to assess its effects without the escapist romanticization of the African past which we find in Camara Laye. The condemnation of colonialism was toned down by a strong ambivalence in the writers' attitude towards the new values which they shared. The concern of these writers has been primarily with the present, which they have tried to assess by dramatizing a dialogue between Western values and the ancestral values of their communities. Achebe's *Things Fall Apart*[25] and *Arrow of God*[26] stand out as the major expositions of this dialogue. Both novels are an interpretation of the first European penetration of Iboland in Eastern Nigeria. In the first novel we see the conflict mainly from the way in which it affects a self-made, ambitious, haughty and reactionary tribal elder. He counsels total war against the strangers but finds himself without the support of his fellow tribesmen, some of whom have already been converted to the doctrines of the strangers. After killing an emissary of the invader he takes his own life. The hero of *Arrow of God* has none of this crusading zeal. He believes in cunning rather than violent confrontation. But his diplomatic ingenuity becomes the source of his undoing. His own son, whom he sends to school as an agent to observe the new religion from inside, is converted and commits a sacrilegious act that leads to a tragic quarrel within the tribe. As in the first novel the tribe is finally left in disarray because the traditional values which are the foundation of the tribal way of life have been infiltrated and undermined by new foreign values. The author is committed neither to condemning nor extolling this infiltration. What is significant in this interpretation of history is that it highlights the fact that the West did not simply have to rely on force to plant its values in Africa. Western values were willingly embraced by many sections of African communities because of inherent weaknesses in traditional cultures. Chinua Achebe's view on the subject, which has been expressed elsewhere,[27] is that all cultures have something to gain from others because cultures are healthy when organic and adaptable. By and large this is the position of many African novelists in English. The colonial experience cannot be entirely rejected. There was much to be gained from the contact with Europe. How much gain and how much loss is still the subject of debate by writers both literary and non-literary.

But just as many writers are taking the view that negritude has outlived its usefulness, so many of them are beginning to see the limitations of seeking an understanding of modern African life through a dialogue between 'ancestral' and Western values. Recent novels are tending to portray the African present as an autonomous experience, without dwelling on the conflicting elements of culture within it.

The discussion so far leads us to see the African novel as a creative interpretation of history, beginning at the time of the colonial occupation of the continent. The most convenient classification of the novel therefore seems to be according to which aspects of this history particular novels depict. There are the novels which deal mainly with the past, or with the beginning of colonialism. There are those which portray the process of colonial domination. There are those which recreate the struggle for independence and there are those which evoke the post-independence social and political climate.

This book has two main aims: first, to provide a critical assessment of twelve major African novels; and secondly, through this assessment, to outline the major concerns of African fiction. It is our hope that the discussion which follows will help the reader to appreciate the more subjective statements which we make in the concluding chapter.

NOTES

1. Césaire, Aimé, 'Culture and Colonization', *Présence Africaine* (special issue), Paris, 1956.
2. Equiano, O., *Interesting Narrative of the Life of Olaudah Equiano, or Gustavus Vassa the African*, London, 1789. (Reprinted in 1967 as *Equiano's Travels*, edited by Paul Edwards, Heinemann, London.)
3. Jahn, Janheinz, *A History of Neo-African Literature*, Faber, London, 1968.
4. Legum, Colin, *Pan-Africanism*, Pall Mall Press, London, 1965.
5. Blyden, Edward, *Christianity, Islam and the Negro Race*, 1887. (Reprinted in 1967, edited by C. Fife, Edinburgh University Press.)
6. Mofolo, Thomas, *Chaka*, transl. by F. H. Dutton, O.U.P., London, 1931.
7. Plaatje, Solomon, *Mhudi*, Lovedale Press (S.A.), 1930.
8. Abrahams, Peter, *Song of the City*, Faber and Faber, London, 1945.
9. Kesteloot, Lilyan, *Les Ecrivains Noirs de Language Française*, Université Libre de Bruxelles, Brussels, 1965.
10. Jahn, Janheinz, *op. cit.*
11. Wauthier, Claude, *The Literature and Thought of Modern Africa*, Pall Mall Press, London, 1966.
12. Le Vine, Victor, *Political Leadership in Africa*, Stanford University Press, 1967.
13. 'Political Protest in the African Novel in English', Rotberg, R. and Mazrui, A. (eds.), *Protest and Power in Black Africa*, Harvard University Centre for International Affairs, New York, 1970, pp. 823–53.
14. 'Ethnology and Negro Culture', *Présence Africaine* (special issue, English edition), Paris, 1956, p. 143.
15. 'Problems of the African Artist Today', *ibid.*, p. 179.
16. *Présence Africaine* (special issue, English edition), Paris, 1959.
17. 'Negritude or Melanism', Legum, Colin and Drysdale, John (eds.), *African Contemporary Record, 1969/70*, Rex Collings, London, pp. 276–86.
18. '*Pan-African Cultural Manifesto*', *Présence Africaine*, no. 71, Paris, 1969, p. 125.
19. *Ibid.*, p. 124.
20. Laurence, Margaret, *Long Drums and Cannons*, Macmillan, London, 1968.
21. For an example, see: 'Writers and Commitment', *Black Orpheus*, vol. 2, no. 3, Ibadan, 1969, pp. 34–9.
22. Mphahlele, Ezekiel, *The African Image*, Faber and Faber, London, 1962, p. 166.
23. La Guma, Alex, *A Walk in the Night*, African Writers Series, Heinemann Educational Books Ltd, London, 1968 (1962).
24. Kane, Cheikh Hamidou, *L'Aventure Ambigue*, René Julliard, Paris, 1962.

25. Achebe, Chinua, *Things Fall Apart,* African Writers Series, Heinemann Educational Books Ltd, London, 1962 (1958).
26. Achebe, Chinua, *Arrow of God,* African Writers Series, Heinemann Educational Books Ltd, London, 1965 (1964).
27. Achebe, Chinua, 'The Black Writer's Burden', *Présence Africaine,* no. 59, Paris, 1962, pp. 135–40.

1. Colonial Injustice

Oyono's *Houseboy*

FOR the execution of its designs colonialism employs both naked force as well as an elaborate apparatus designed to incarcerate the minds of its victims. The latter weapon is the more effective of the two because it takes the victims unawares. Ferdinand Oyono's novels split the two cotyledons of colonialism to uncover the smothered victims struggling painfully towards social and spiritual freedom.

In a nutshell that is what *Houseboy** is about. It is novel about conversion —the painful conversion of the willing and faithful servant of colonialism to passionate anger and bitter renunciation of his innocent complicity in the suffering of his people. With wit and subtlety Oyono presents a microcosm of the colonial situation in the private life of a houseboy.

Joseph Toundi starts his houseboy career with naive expectations of advancement from his white patrons, with naive faith in the Whitemans' benevolence. He willingly gives devoted service to his masters but this devotion is never rewarded let alone reciprocated. For all that he does, he earns humiliation, physical suffering and finally death.

However, before he dies, Toundi awakens to the fact that he has been a victim of a great deception and withdraws his faith in his white 'benefactors'. He dies a rebel and through this rebellion, harmless as it is, he rehabilitates his personal integrity. He is glad to die in Spanish Guinea, out of the way of his treacherous masters.

It is this complete reversal of attitudes and the experience that makes it possible that forms the subject of the novel. Toundi's disillusion comes through a slow and painful process which we begin to perceive clearly when we start reading the second exercise book of his notes. By the end of the first notebook we are no longer listening to the simple-minded and trusting Toundi of the beginning. There is a touch of cynicism in his style. At the beginning Toundi introduces himself as follows:

*Oyono, Ferdinand, *Houseboy*, African Writers Series, Heinemann Educational Books Ltd, London, 1966 (1960). (Page references are to the reset 1975 edition.)

> My name is Toundi Ondoua. I am the son of Toundi and Zama. When the father baptized me he gave me the name of Joseph. I am Maka by my mother and Ndjem by my father. My ancestors were cannibals. Since the white men came we have learnt other men must not be looked upon as animals. (p. 9)

Here we see the mind of a child recording 'facts' which it has innocently assimilated. The young mind is puzzled by its experience and naively accepts whatever the white man says. At the beginning of the second notebook, we hear a different voice. Toundi is positively groping towards understanding his world:

> In Dangan the European quarter and the African quarter are quite separate. But what goes on under those corrugated-iron roofs is known down to the smallest detail inside the mud-walled huts. The eyes that live in the native location strip the whites naked. The whites on the other hand go about blind. There was not a soul unaware that the wife of the Commandant was deceiving her husband with M. Moreau the prison-director and our greatest terror. (p. 71)

Here Toundi is not recording things that he has been told by someone else. He is making an observation which shows a more mature view of the intricacies of social relationships within the Dangan community. This particular entry is a simple observation that exposes the ugly truths of the colonial social set-up. Toundi's stay with the white man is an apprenticeship that yields a greater understanding and a clearer perception of his situation as a member of a subjugated and oppressed community.

In the earlier part of the novel Toundi suffers without realizing that he is suffering. He takes it for granted that he should be kicked, insulted, overworked and underpaid. He does not react to the unfairness implied in the relationship that exists between him and his masters. He is a keen observer who records his experience because he is puzzled by it. Indeed it is Toundi's bewilderment and his insensitivity to the cruelty which is daily served to him that often provides the comic butt to the story.

> Now I am at St. Peter's Catholic Mission at Dangan. I wake up every morning at five o'clock and even earlier sometimes when all the priests are at the Mission. I ring the little bell hung at the entrance to the sacristy, then I wait for the first father to come for Mass. I serve up to three or four Masses every day. The skin on my knees is now as hard as crocodile skin. When I kneel down I seem to be kneeling on cushions. (p. 17)

Toundi's simplicity and naivety is made a vehicle of Oyono's acute irony. The young houseboy is made to record his experience with pride instead of bitterness. His attitude is a result of the systematic brainwashing to which he has been subjected by his master, Father Gilbert. The relationship between the master and the servant is brought out in entries such as this one:

> Everything I am I owe to Father Gilbert. He is my benefactor and I am very fond of him. He is cheerful and pleasant and when I was small he treated me like a pet animal. He loved to pull my ears and all the time I have been getting my education he has loved to watch my constant amazement at everything.
>
> He presents me to the whites who visit the Mission as his masterpiece. I am his boy, a boy who can read and write, serve Mass, lay a table, sweep out his room and make his bed. I don't earn any money. Now and then he gives me an old shirt or an old pair of trousers. Father Gilbert knew me when I was stark naked, he taught me to read and write . . . Nothing can be more precious than that, even if I have to go badly dressed. (pp. 14–15)

Toundi has been taught to hate himself and his colour. His contact with Christianity has conditioned him to believe that everything good comes from the whites and that everything black is primitive. He hopes to live a better and more civilized life through his contact with the white man.

The principal motive which leads Toundi into the service of Father Gilbert is sheer infantile curiosity

> Father Gilbert believes it was the Holy Spirit that led me to him. In fact I just wanted to get close to the white man with hair like the beard on a maize cob who dressed in woman's clothes and gave little black boys sugar lumps. (p. 9)

However, beneath this curiosity lies an assumption which is inevitable in a child brought up under colonial rule: white men are better people than blacks. This is the assumption which decoys him and many of his countrymen into spending their lifetimes trying to turn themselves into Frenchmen. Little do they understand that in so doing they are betraying their own community as well as their humanity. For the sensitive members of the community this situation is a source of great bitterness. It is the wounded pride of Toundi's father when he sees Father Gilbert throwing lumps of sugar to African children that results in his cruelty against the son. Later, the father ingratiates himself before the son and priest in a desperate attempt at reconciliation but instead the son puts out his tongue at him. The father walks away in bitterness, 'crestfallen'.

It is significant that Toundi runs away from his family on the eve of initiation. By going to the Catholic mission he chooses another form of initiation—one in which he is to play the role of a pet animal, and later the beast of burden.

When Father Gilbert dies things change drastically for Toundi. Since he no longer has the option of returning to his community he has to look for a job within the white community. During his interview with Commandant Decazy for a job we realize that Toundi has already changed a great deal. He has learnt to tell lies to the white man because that is the only way to find favour with him. It is because he pretends to be religious that he gets a servant's job. His stay at the commandant's house eventually opens his eyes to the fact that white men are not the gods he thought they were. When the commandant's wife starts sleeping with the prison officer, M. Moreau, Toundi finds it difficult to hide his contempt and feeling of moral superiority over her. Every time he meets her a faint smile develops at the corner of his mouth. This, together with the somewhat bizarre reaction to the discovery that the commandant is not circumcized, leads Toundi to feel a moral superiority over the whites and thereafter he is no longer awed by them. Because the masters are aware that the servant has begun to find fault with their life they feel he is a threat to their security. It becomes implicitly agreed that he must be got rid of. Kalisia's advice to Toundi makes explicit the reason why the white community has to destroy Toundi:

> 'I was saying though, that because you know all their business, while you are still here, they can never forget about it altogether. And they will never forgive you for that. How can they go on strutting about with a cigarette in their mouth in front of you—when you *know*. As far as they are concerned you are the one who has told everybody and they can't help feeling you are sitting in judgement on them. But that they can never accept .... If I were in your shoes, I'd go right away.... I wouldn't even wait for my month's wages.' (pp. 100–1)

But his habitual loyalty keeps him on until he reaps its bitter reward—death.

Although Toundi is the centre of interest throughout the novel, other African characters are introduced, mainly to act as foils to his actions. His father's bitterness and feeling of insult at what the whites are doing to his community are contrasted with the son's dreams of being friends with the white man. The mother's words of warning against greed are recalled many times in the novel. While the chiefs of Dangan are all obliged to attend ceremonies and pay their respects to the whiteman there is a lot of difference in the enthusiasm with which they do this. Akoma, the chief of the Sos, is always the first to arrive, and he has been rewarded for this enthusiasm with a trip to France from where he has brought five golden rings referred to as 'alliances'. On the other hand, Menguene, the chief of the Yanyas, wears European clothes only when he is in the European town.

Otherwise he wears traditional robes. He is more respected by his people than the other chiefs.

The other domestic servants are more important foils to Toundi's behaviour. Baklu, the cook, claims that he is hardly ever likely to come into conflict with the white man because he does exactly and only what his masters expect him to do. He says to Toundi:

> 'Toundi will you never learn what a houseboy's job is? One of these days you'll be the cause of real trouble. When will you grasp that for the whites, you are only alive to do their work and for no other reason. I am the cook. The white man does not see me except with his stomach. (p. 87)

This is the kind of relationship which Toundi revolts against.

The character who exhibits even more important differences with Toundi is Sophie, the mistress of the agricultural engineer. She is the bitterest of all the characters in the novel. She seems to be always in tears, regularly breaking out into the simple question: 'Christ what have other women got that I haven't got?' The agricultural engineer, who is privately fond of her and extremely jealous about her, calls her his cook when in the presence of other whites. This embitters her so much that her life becomes a search for revenge. Eventually an opportunity does come. She gains access to 150,000 francs with which she runs away to Spanish Guinea. In her view she meets the whites on their terms.

All these different reactions to foreign rule enable us to understand better Toundi's own dreams of being a friend of the white man, the consequences that follow from this folly and finally his discovery of the truth.

After Toundi's arrest events move hurriedly towards the tragic end. He is interrogated, tortured, starved and finally mortally wounded. The consensus, or at least connivance to get rid of Toundi, demonstrates the sense of insecurity which drives the colonial community at Dangan to practise the mean brutalities against the blacks. It is the herd instinct—which has been so penetratingly described in E. M. Forster's *Passage to India*—that breeds uncritical attitudes which in turn breed narrow-mindedness and crass behaviour. Evidence of this can be seen in the hostility expressed towards M. Salvain, the school teacher, who is charged with spoiling natives by telling his school children that they are as good as whites. The Dangan whites spend their time idling, gossiping and drinking and yet they never cease to boast about their 'civilizing mission' in Africa.

Because of the attitude of the whites there is no real contact between them and the society in the middle of which they live. The two communities live side by side without communication except through kicks, whips, slaps and insulting commands. Nothing but mistrust exists between the two colour groups. We see this in Father Vandermayer who never lets his African assistants take the Sunday collection. Out of necessity, however, one day he lets Toundi take the collection. Afterwards he takes Toundi to his room, undresses him and searches him. He then makes one of the catechists stay with Toundi throughout the day just in case the latter has swallowed any of the coins! Another incident which illustrates the same absurd suspicion is when Sophie's lover swears to take her to the hospital after she has accidentally slept in the same hut with Toundi.

In Dangan, life is strictly segregated—including church services and cemeteries. This segregation is designed to protect the image which the whites believe they project to the natives, little knowing that the natives see through their pretences. Any native who is discovered to be knowing what he is not supposed to know has to pay a very heavy price—probably his life, as happens in the case of Toundi. Everything takes place against a background of suspicion and misunderstanding and this background underlies both the humour and the tragedy of the novel. Although Toundi lives within the white community he is never admitted into it beyond the physical fact. He therefore views the life of the white man from the outside. Sometimes he confesses his failure to interpret their gestures and sometimes we see the whites misinterpreting the gestures of the blacks. The turning point in the war of nerves between Madame Decazy and Toundi comes when the latter is seen turning rubber tubes in the bedroom with a broom. Toundi does not know that they are contraceptives but his mistress misunderstands the gesture and flares up. This is how Toundi records this incident in his diary:

> There are times when the anger of the white people leaves you completely blank. While all this was going on I did not understand anything. Madame pushed me outside and I stood completely bewildered on the veranda. (p. 86)

Toundi is made to learn simple things through bitter and harsh experience, to learn serious things through comic incidents and to miss other things through his ignorance—as the whites miss a lot of things through their arrogance. And it is because of this arrogance that they finally kill him for his knowledge.

Houseboy is among other things a novel about childhood, growth and discovery. It is about the various phases of a child's reaction to his social environment. The novel explores the slow but inevitable awakening of the child's mind to the realities of the colonial situation. Throughout we see the society tending to obstruct rather than assist the child's mental development and as a result of the numerous obstacles to his understanding

Toundi never makes any moral appraisal of his situation until it is too late for him to make any practical remedies. He dies with a deep sense of regret because his entire life has been a waste. The only thing he can do is mentally to reject his past which he has no opportunity to reconstruct.

It is in the portrayal of the child's development that the novel shows some lapses of control. The subtleties of the child's moods are effectively captured but some entries fail to reflect the general pattern of the main character's mental development. At the beginning when Toundi records that Father Gilbert treats him like a pet animal and that he presents him to other whites as his masterpiece there is a suggestion of an awareness which we do not see sometime later when Toundi says somewhat innocently: 'I shall be the chief European's boy. The dog of the king is the king of dogs.' One might suppose that the very choice of this proverb implies some irony but then one cannot reconcile the suggested cynicism with Toundi's innocent ecstasy when much later he shakes hands for the first time with the commandant's wife:

> My happiness has neither day nor night. I didn't know about it, it just burst upon my whole being. I will sing to my flute, I will sing on the banks of rivers, but no words can express my happiness. I have held the hand of my queen. I felt that I was really alive. From now on my hand is sacred and must not know the lower regions of my body. (p. 47)

Nevertheless a clear pattern of mental development does emerge and Toundi gains ever-increasing knowledge until in his own words the job of houseboy holds no more secrets for him. The logical end of this process of discovery is the moment of truth which comes just before death. We see him develop from the early time of gratitude for being allowed to get close to the white man, to the time when he calls himself 'the thing that obeys', to the time of lies, to the time when he looks white men in the face and refuses to cry when they beat him. Then, inevitably, open hostility develops between him and his masters and they do their best to crack his sense of superiority but they fail. What makes him even more unbearable in the eyes of his persecutors is the fact that the more violence they practise on him the more contempt he shows them. When they arrest him they set to work upon him through African warders who crack his ribs with rifle butts until, in the words of the hospital orderly, he is only good for Spanish Guinea or the prison cemetery. He takes a desperate chance to flee to Spanish Guinea but falls unconscious at the border. Later he regains consciousness for a little while in the company of his rescuers. It is then that he utters to the narrator a clear statement of renunciation of his connections with French colonialists. In between gasps and coughing of blood he is made wise by his bitterness and he declares: '. . . I'd have made old bones if I'd been good and stayed at home in the village.'

The recurrence of animal imagery throughout the novel crystallizes into new meaning when Toundi is turned into an offering for the unity of the whites. The decadent life the whites lead and their lack of contact with any living culture that might restrain them from bestial competition among themselves requires that from time to time they should invoke the native menace to bring about temporary harmony. When the white community is threatened with personal quarrels and jealousies Toundi is turned into a convenient scapegoat against whom all hatreds are directed. His liquidation brings about a temporary patching up of differences. Toundi's blood is shed so that unity might be restored among the conquerors. The extensive complicity is a ritualized perennial act of group defence.

The novel is a remarkable experiment in fictional form and a number of structural and stylistic ingenuities which it employs to make its statement are worth noting.

To begin with there is the sustained impression of eavesdropping upon an experience which was never intended for the reader to know about. For the protagonist, an emotionally emasculated domestic servant who is alienated from his tribal community and ignored by his masters, the diary is invented as a private outlet of feeling because he is too shy to express his innermost thoughts to anybody. The diary is discovered by accident and translated by someone who recognizes its value. This device makes credible the reader's access to the innermost feelings of a socially withdrawn personality.

Secondly, the novel opens with the death of the protagonist. The reader therefore is not a direct witness of the events which make up the fictional experience. The events are distanced in time and this makes it possible for the reader to accept the presentation of an essentially tragic experience in humorous terms. This is perhaps the most remarkable quality of the novel: the subtle blending of humour and tragedy.

Thirdly, we never hear the voice of the author. All entries in the diary are the subjective views of their author. Therefore, we are not to expect a literary style, or a logical organization of experience. The short disjointed sentences are a more credible style for a houseboy who has had no formal education. This contributes to the willing suspension of disbelief.

Lastly, the presence of the translator—whose role is between that of a Greek chorus and of a modern fictional narrator—who is also a fugitive from the same menace of colonial injustice is turned into ingenuous evidence that Toundi's experience is not an isolated one. We are told by the translator that there are many such fugitives running away from the common terror to find temporary respite or their death-bed in Spanish Guinea. The very interest the translator takes in the diary is evidence that it speaks for him too. Between the sullied pages of Toundi's notebooks he reads his own life. Thus, while Toundi is very much an individual he is at the same time a representative figure. Moreover, the translator serves to fill in the gap in the story between the moment when Toundi loses consciousness and the time when the diary is published. Our interest is aroused in the notebooks and their author before we actually start reading them.

When Toundi poses the question, 'What are we? What are we black men who are called French?' the narrator gapes at the dying man hiccupping blood and feels stupefied because he has never asked himself that question. And this is Toundi's triumph which makes worthwhile all his suffering. He is at last able to pose that question to his fellow so-called black Frenchmen. Indeed his whole diary moves towards the posing of that question. The narrator recognizes the importance of that question and because of this he translates and publishes Toundi's diary. This diary vindicates Toundi as someone whose life is not wasted by the conquerors of his people. His experience of servitude enables him to make a record and leave behind him a document that exposes the system which has killed him.

Human suffering is subject matter common to literature of all cultures. In the African context, colonial oppression—the suffering of the subject and the brutality of the conqueror—has attracted the imagination of many artists and it is perhaps the recurrence of this theme that earned African literature the once popular label of 'protest literature'.

Effective presentation of suffering has to avoid cataloguing injustices, physical brutalities and moral rage of the victims. It is the journalistic fact and sociological fact which so often stultify fictional experiments into mere documentary. In *Houseboy*, through acute subtlety and stinging humour Oyono has given form to ordinary facts and made a forceful and truthful statement about an important aspect of modern African life. No African novel has portrayed the realities of colonialism so memorably.

La Guma's *A Walk in the Night*

South African critics have often complained about the failure of their writers to respond meaningfully to the complex dilemmas of their society. The charge has been made frequently that most South African writers adopt conventional plots which either illustrate the arbitrary nature of the police system and usually end in petty gestures of defiance in the name of the universal brotherhood of man or some other admirable moral sentiment.

While this is a fair general criticism and while it is true that black South African literature suffers from the return again and again to the same old theme of apartheid, we should acknowledge the existence of a few writers who have treated this theme with sufficient originality to make a universally valid statement about the human condition.

Few works have treated this theme with the same freshness which we find in Alex La Guma's *A Walk in the Night**. What distinguishes this short novel is that while avoiding being a sermon of despair it also avoids advocating sentimental solutions to the problems that it portrays. Without pathos, it creates a powerful impression of that rhythm of violence which characterizes South African life.

The novel opens with a rather frightening scene in which a young man recklessly jumps off a moving truck and throws himself in the middle of a busy street. He ignores the horns and the curses of the drivers and dodges through the traffic until he reaches the pavement. Here begins his evening of aimless walking from café to café, smoking cheap cigarettes, drinking cheap wine and quarrelling. Earlier in the day he has lost his job because he returned the insult of a white factory boss. The young man keeps swearing 'I'll get him', but deep down he knows he won't and because of this frustration he commits a pointless murder that same evening.

Michael Adonis' wanderings which culminate in the killing of Doughty, a retired actor, his escape from the police and the immediate effect of this experience upon his life, form the central plot of the novel. Subplots develop as Michael Adonis crosses at different points 'the unending flow of derelicts, bums, loungers, domestic workers off duty, loiterers, FAH-FEE numbers runners, petty gangsters, thugs'—and of course the police.

The principal walkers in the night are Michael Adonis, Raalt, the white constable who is on patrol duty in Cape Town's District Six and Willieboy, a habitual loiterer and petty criminal who gets killed by Raalt during the hunt for the murderer of Doughty. As the lives of these people cross each other during the night they meet a wide range of District dwellers. All these bar-tenders, drunkards, loungers, sailors and labourers are in some way or another victims of 'the foul crimes' of their society.

Doughty, the old drunkard ex-actor, speaks for numerous members of his society when he recites the words from *Hamlet*:

* La Guma, Alex, *A Walk in the Night*, African Writers Series, Heinemann Educational Books Ltd, London, 1968 (1962).

> I am thy father's spirit, doomed for a certain time to walk the night . . . and . . . and for the day confined to fast in fires, till the foul crimes done in my days of natures . . . nature are burnt and purged away. . . .' (p. 28)

This retired actor who is dying of alcoholism, diabetes and old age, before he is finished off by Michael Adonis, has once been a famous man. Now he is left trapped in the *atelier* of a derelict tenement waiting for death which comes even sooner than expected. The very description of his room gives it a deathly quality.

> The room was hot and airless as a newly opened tomb, and there was an old iron bed against one wall, covered with unwashed bedding, and next to it a backless chair that served as a table on which stood a chipped ashtray full of cigarette butts and burnt matches, and a thick tumbler, sticky with the dregs of heavy red wine. A battered cupboard stood in a corner with cracked, fly spotted mirror over it, and a small stack of dog-eared books gathering dust. (pp. 24–5)

And as complement to the deathly air the inhabitant of the room looks like a ghost:

> In the light of the bulb in the ceiling his face looked yellowish-blue. The purple-veined, greyish skin had loosened all over it and sagged in blotched, puffy folds. With his sagging lower eyelids, revealing blood-shot rims, and the big, bulbous, red-veined nose that had once been aquiline, his face had the expression of a decrepit bloodhound. His head was almost bald, and wisps of dirty grey hair clung to the bony, pinkish skull like scrub clinging to eroded rock. (p. 24)

When Doughty recalls the words of the ghost in *Hamlet* he is recalling them for all the characters in the novel, all of whom, in one way or another, experience the terrors of the South African night, where in a life punctuated by violent encounters, imprisonments and murders, the people fast in fires of hatred, fear and frustration.

The rhythm of life in District Six, Cape Town, is one of violence, and the incidents, the language and imagery of the novel are carefully chosen to give the reader a lasting impression of this harsh rhythm. Michael Adonis, the protagonist is described as 'trailing his tattered raincoat behind him like a sword-slashed, bullet-ripped banner just rescued from battle'. Wherever he goes he seems to be involved in a desperate fight in which he is doomed to lose. As soon as he loses his job he becomes a potential recruit for the gangster groups that roam the streets of Cape Town. He spends most of the evening dodging and resisting the urgings of the petty criminals who want to assign 'jobs' to him. Before the night is over he has succumbed to their urging and sets off with one of the gangs 'to fix some job'.

Willieboy is addicted to habitual violence. To the gangster groups who want to recruit him he says: 'No, man, me I don't work. Never worked a bogger yet. Whether you work or don't, you live anyway, somehow. I haven't starved to death, have I? Work. Eff work.' (p. 4). With a knife in his pocket he is always wandering aimlessly, getting involved in quarrels and fights and occasionally robbing men who are weaker than himself. We see him knocking down a harmless drunkard, Mr Green, picking a quarrel with sailors in a café and finally we see him dying violently.

Police constable Raalt is perhaps the most sharply drawn figure in the novel. He is the incarnation of the fears and complexes of the white man in South Africa. He is a dehumanized instrument of supremacy and terror.

Raalt is frustrated by nights of boredom, of driving around on patrol, armed to the teeth, without locating the enemy. He wants to come to grips with something which can absorb his anger against the failure of his marriage. His wife has grown seedy, dull and boring and she no longer cares for him. What Raalt would really like to do is 'wring her bloody neck' but he is afraid of possible consequences. She is a white woman. Raalt is therefore compelled to transfer his aggression to the non-whites, the necks of whom he can wring without any fear of consequences. 'I wish something would happen,' he says. 'I'd like to lay my hands on one of those bushman bastards and wring his bloody neck.' And with this urge driving him he goes around bullying non-whites in the bars and on the road until the discovery of Doughty's dead body gives him the opportunity to fulfil his wish. His inquiries are rough and hurried. As soon as he learns that there was a man in a yellow shirt who ran out of the corridor of Doughty's tenement he decides to get hold of any coloured in a yellow shirt. He embarks on the chase with brutal efficiency and does not rest until he has shot Willieboy twice in the chest.

The way Raalt, Adonis and Willieboy live through the evening shows parallel transfers of aggression. All these characters are victims of a system that denies them the facility of living in harmony with fellow human beings and their frustrations find release in acts of violence against weaker members of their society. Their failure to see themselves as integral parts of any living community is their plight to which the novel suggests no solution. Hence the sense of doom which overhangs the novel.

The background against which the events are narrated suggests an atmosphere that is hostile to the well-being of man. La Guma often relies on the careful building up of physical detail to characterize the environment in which the action of the novel takes place. The tenements of the coloured community in Cape Town are the main scene of action and it is the physical disintegration of the buildings, the filth and dampness which surround them as well as the scavenging insects which inhabit the dark corners that give the life in these tenements its special character. The physical violence and decay of the whole area becomes the objective correlative of the moral and social disintegration of South African society. Note, for example, the effective use of the description of a street as Michael Adonis walks through it:

> He turned down another street, away from the artificial glare of Hanover, between stretches of damp, battered houses with their broken-ribs of front-railings; cracked walls and high tenements that rose like the left-overs of a bombed area in the twilight; vacant lots and weed-grown patches where houses had once stood; and deep doorways resembling the entrances to deserted castles. There were children playing in the street, darting among the over-flowing dustbins and shooting at each other with wooden guns. In some of the doorways people sat or stood, murmuring idly in the fast-fading light like wasted ghosts in a plague-ridden city. (p. 21)

This description recalls the harsh and desolate world of La Guma's *The Stone Country*[1]. The cumulative images of violence, sickness and war are used to emphasize the material discomfort and harshness of the environment in which the people live. The very games that the children play is evidence of the disorientation which is bound to result from living in such conditions. The sights, the sounds and the smells are used to give a powerful impression of the conditions in which the people live.

The episodic and disjointed character of the plot is part of the author's means of emphasizing the separateness of groups and individuals within the society. The sub-plots are loosely linked to the main plot. The lives of Raalt, Willieboy, Joe and Michael Adonis only cross accidently. They do not form one coherent story. This device of multiple sub-plots sometimes threatens narrative continuity by giving the impression of arbitrariness as the author tries to keep our attention, simultaneously, on a number of episodes which at first seem unrelated. But the shortness of the work together with the vigour and pace of narration ensure that there is no moment of boredom.

It is also part of the overall design of the novel that there should be no resolution at the end. We are not interested in the life of one individual but in the lives of many individuals whose connection is that they are oppressed by the same system. The author makes the lives of these characters cross, but when they have crossed, each goes his own way to lead his own different life. They all remain lonely walkers in the night. The crossing of these different lives creates memorable impressions of urban life in South

Africa and through these impressions the author bears witness not only against the apartheid system but against the oppression of class rule everywhere.

NOTE

1. La Guma, Alex, *The Stone Country*, African Writers Series, Heinemann Educational Books Ltd, London, 1974 (1967).

2. The Illusion of Progress

Achebe's *No Longer at Ease*

ONE of the ways by which the novel has offered criticism of modern African life is by showing the falseness behind commonly accepted assumptions of progress. Chinua Achebe's *No Longer at Ease** does this and sets out to assess, in broad terms, the colonial inheritance of Nigeria on the eve of the country's independence. The action is centred on a patriotic but in some ways naive young graduate who aspires to rid his country of moral and social ills which he attributes to backwardness. Slowly, as his enthusiasm becomes eroded by the temptations of privilege and the stresses of living in a decaying social system, he succumbs to a deep pessimism and acknowledges the inadequacy of his generation in providing answers to the complex dilemmas of modern Africa.

Obi Okonkwo is a representative of the African intelligentsia which, on the eve of independence, looked upon itself—and was looked upon by the ex-colonial powers, as well as by the masses of Africa—as the natural leaders of the new society. His life is deliberately conventionalized. He is no revolutionary. He is someone who has done well at school, become the pride of his tribe and won a scholarship from them to study in England. While in England his nationalistic sentiments are awakened. He makes some petty speeches at student union meetings and writes a few sentimental poems about his fatherland. When he comes home he gets a job in the civil service. The laudable ideals that he formulated at student meetings in England are carefully tucked away in a briefcase.

For a man of such laudable ideals the very choice of a civil service career suggests unacknowledged insincerity or naivety and this is one of the ways in which the author invites us to view the hero with irony. Obi does not recognize the contradictions of his life style until he goes through painful experiences that bring him into conflict with his fianceé, his family, his tribe

*Achebe, Chinua, *No Longer at Ease*, African Writers Series, Heinemann Educational Books Ltd, London, 1963 (1960). (Page references are to the reset 1975 edition.)

and the law, as well as with his own ideals. His disillusionment is expressed in the symbolic tearing up of 'Nigeria', the poem he wrote in Britain two years earlier.

The first stanza of this poem exemplifies well the dreamy, euphoristic quality of Obi's nationalistic sentiments and this is contextualized in such a way as to make clear the author's judgement of his character:

> God bless our noble fatherland
> Great land of sunshine bright,
> Where brave men chose the way of peace,
> To win their freedom fight.
> May we preserve our purity,
> Our zest for life and jollity. (p. 136)

Two years after writing this poem Obi goes back home. His contact with reality starts him on a process of disillusionment which is completed when he destroys the poem. He does not find in Nigeria either 'the way of peace', 'our purity' or 'zest for life and jollity' expressed in his feeble verse. The destruction of this poem is a gesture towards the renunciation of the facile dream. But even after this Obi does not show much ability to face up to the reality of his situation. When he renounces his sentimental dream he allows himself to fall into a deep cynicism: he takes bribes, is arrested, tried and sent to prison. We find it difficult to give him our full sympathy, and the author himself seems to invite pity at best. Obi gives in too easily. The betrayal of his original principles remains unmitigated by any dignity or irony of motive. He takes a bribe merely to keep up appearances as a member of the affluent élite who are busy maintaining their cars and paying back the loans for their education. Towards the end of the novel his attitude towards money and appearances has completely changed from what it was when he first arrived back from England when, though the Umuofia Progressive Union had booked a room for him in an expensive hotel, he refused to use it and stayed with an old friend, a clerk in Lagos. However, gradually he surrenders to the influence of a sterile social system and his actions illustrate moral degeneration. We are often impatient with his smugness. His hatred of the social ills which he sees around him does not move him to any positive action. He is content with an occasional condemnation of the system during his discussions with Christopher, a cynical lawyer who is devoted to making money. Otherwise he is content with merely personal and rather complacent abstention from corruption. One might have expected a man of his convictions and in his position to have made a more positive effort. But he lacks the daring to rise to any kind of social commitment. He does not even spare more than occasional moments to reflect on the problems of his country and when he does so he snows lack of depth. His lack of seriousness is illustrated by his reaction to the incident in which a policeman takes a bribe from a taxi driver in the presence of many passengers, including Obi. All the other passengers accept the arrangement and blame Obi for having embarrassed the policeman with a stare. As nobody is willing to speak to him for the rest of the journey he falls into thought which displays his characteristic superficiality.

> 'What an Augean stable!' he muttered to himself. 'Where does one begin? With the masses? Educate the masses?' He shook his head. 'Not a chance there. It would take centuries. A handful of men at the top. Or even one man with vision—an enlightened dictator. People are scared of the word nowadays. But what kind of democracy can exist side by side with so much corruption and ignorance? Perhaps a half-way house—a sort of compromise.' When Obi's reasoning reached this point he reminded himself that England had been as corrupt not so very long ago. He was not really in the mood for consecutive reasoning. His mind was impatient to roam in a more pleasant landscape. (p. 40)

In fact Obi is never in the mood for consecutive reasoning. What the passage illustrates is his unwillingness to come to grips with his situation in a mature, responsible and committed manner. His mind contemplates the most obvious solutions, and when he realizes their inadequacy he abandons the effort and is soon absorbed in his financial problems. And yet he is willing to condemn the less educated people for their ignorance. Obi's behaviour becomes an indictment of the privileged élite who wish to see things running in the best way possible but are unwilling to make any sacrifices that might initiate change. As the novel progresses we realise that Obi's so-called patriotism is only a sentimental indulgence cultivated in moments of loneliness while he was living abroad. Once he returns to Nigeria he gets increasingly absorbed with personal problems, many of which are imaginary. The implications of Obi's character for the novelist's own artistic control have been pointed out by Arthur Ravenscroft in his discussion of *No Longer at Ease*. He states:

> While this story can also be read partly as a paradigm of a man caught between the irreconcilable values of different ways of life, his enmeshment happens too easily to win our sympathetic involvement. As the catalogue of debts and expenditure mounts, one becomes too aware of the cards being stacked against him. It is a very simple-minded young man indeed who does not expect to receive a demand for income tax or an electricity bill.[1]

Indeed sometimes Obi appears inexplicably simple-minded, which makes him an inadequate expression of the social conflict of his society. He allows himself to be overwhelmed by his problems. He makes no attempt to bridge the wide gap between his idealism and the social reality which confronts him. He is the impatient idealist whom the author reminds us asks for a place to stand on in order to move the earth. But the author also reminds us that there is no such place and that 'we all have to stand on the earth itself and go with her at her pace'.

Obi's principal call is to rid his country's public service of corruption. He likes to think that he has a consistent theory of how to cure the country of this evil. The naivety of this theory is indicated by the way the author describes it:

> Obi's theory that the public service of Nigeria would remain corrupt until the old Africans at the top were replaced by young men from the universities was first formulated in a paper read to the Nigerian Students' Union in London. But unlike most theories formed by students in London, this one survived the first impact of homecoming. (p. 35)

Whereas it is common for African students abroad to invent simple theories to solve all the problems of their countries, in Obi's case he clings to these naive theories after his return to Nigeria, even though he realizes that his original picture of the country was a false one. On the very day of arrival in his 'noble fatherland', the first Nigerian he meets, a customs official, tries to extract a bribe from him. He refuses to pay the bribe and has to bear with the rough treatment which is meted out to him as a result. While he is waiting for an employment interview with the Public Service Commission, all his friends advise him to go and 'see' some highly placed official in the government because this is the accepted way of getting jobs in Nigeria. However, because he is going into the senior service he escapes having to endure the same process of self-ingratiation as his fellow-Nigerians. As soon as he has got the job of secretary to the scholarship commission he receives an endless line of clients offering bribes for back-door entry to scholarship awards. One of the female candidates for a scholarship goes to the extent of offering to sleep with Obi, but Clara arrives at the house in time to save him from yielding to the temptation.

No Longer at Ease is among many recent novels which try to show that corruption is one of the greatest problems facing the new African states. It also shows how this malpractice becomes entangled with other social evils. Nepotism is one which exists inseparably side by side with bribery. The man who comes to offer a bribe to Obi in the latter's office expects special treatment because he is an Ibo. A policeman who is harassing people on the beach apologizes to Obi when he finds out that he is an Ibo like himself.

The moral deterioration of the society is reflected by the fact that a girl is willing to sleep with a man in return for assistance to gain a scholarship and that policemen find it necessary to patrol beaches in the evenings to check on rich car-owners having affairs with other people's wives. These things testify to a general breakdown of a moral order which the traditional society was able, for various reasons, to maintain. As a result unhealthy social relationships develop and are generally accepted. The extent to which all the institutions of society are abused is reflected in the public reaction to Obi's trial. We are told that 'some civil servants paid as much as ten shillings and sixpence to obtain a doctor's certificate of illness for the day' in order to attend the trial which is a challenge to the system of which they are part. Only the colonial officials blame Obi on moral grounds. Most other people blame him for not having taken the necessary precautions against being caught. Some Umuofians say that he should have accepted the bribe through his cook. Others blame him for having fallen for so small a bribe. They argue that it would have been more respectable to get caught taking a substantial bribe.

The socially destructive forces which lead to the breakdown of order in *A Man of the People*[2] were anticipated in this novel, which appeared six years earlier. In the latter novel the emphasis is on the behaviour of the politicians while in the earlier one the emphasis was on the social values which are the foundation of the political life of the country. In portraying the malaise which afflicted Nigerian society on the eve of independence, Achebe was trying to examine the underlying structural weaknesses of the system on which the new society was being built and to call for a revaluation of the social patterns evolved during the colonial era. The concept of Nigeria as one nation is shown to be less real than appears on the surface. Each small group is pursuing its own interests largely in disregard of other groups. This theme is to be developed later in *A Man of the People* where the attitude of the common people towards the new nation is shown to be the same as that of children towards a cake from which each demands a share. In *No Longer at Ease*, at the party which the Umuofia Progressive Union organizes to welcome Obi back from England the chairman of the party asks him: 'have *they* given you a job yet?' And the author explains to us:

> In Nigeria the government was 'they'. It had nothing to do with you or me. It was an alien institution and people's business was to get as much out of it as they could without getting into trouble. (pp. 29–30)

Ironically, even Obi's attitude is only superficially different. He objects to corruption only as long as he has enough to live on. When he starts work with the civil service he resents the way he is treated by his boss, Mr Green, and the fact that he is made to share a room with a stenographer. But because he wants a secure job in the civil service he stomachs the scorn of

Green and his complaints against the system slowly diminish. When he gets into financial difficulties he tries to claim as many allowances as he can. On one occasion he locks himself up in his Lagos house over a weekend so that he might be able to claim a local leave allowance for travelling home. His mentality is typical of the privileged class of the colonial élite who pay lip-service to the interests of the people while in practice they work for their own. Obi's friend, Christopher, is an even more thorough-going self-seeker. We also hear from Green of a Nigerian student in Britain who wrote to his government asking why it did not pay allowances to students' fiancées. Thus Obi's theory that the public service can be set right by replacing the old men with young graduates, is shown dramatically, to be hopelessly inadequate. Their behaviour shows no greater devotion to the community than that of their less educated countrymen. The expatriate civil servant who is the link between the old administration and the new one is so cynical about the whole idea of Africans ruling themselves that he cannot be relied upon to help the young civil servants to develop a sense of responsibility. When Obi is arrested for taking a bribe the old colonial officials regard this as confirmation of their old prejudices: 'they are all corrupt.'

The masses in Achebe's novels always appear bewildered by events and resigned to their fate. The villagers in *Things Fall Apart*[3] gave themselves up to the mercy of the gods and everybody's estate is supposed to have been determined by his *chi*. They do not expect to alter their world. They embrace whatever promises them security, and are not slow to adopt the new religion. In *Arrow of God*[4] it is the poor people who are the first to suffer from famine when the yam harvest is delayed. Consequently they are the first to seek the necessary blessing for their yams from the priests of the new religion. In *No Longer at Ease* the villagers show a remarkable power of adjustment to the demands of Lagos. They do not hope to exercise any influence in the affairs of the city, they are ready to do whatever is required of them so that they can get money to take back to their village. They are very defensive as a group and they behave as if they were on foreign territory. The affairs of the nation are not their concern.

No Longer at Ease has often been discussed in terms of the language which the author uses to portray the hybrid culture of modern Africa.* One of the things on which Achebe's reputation rests is his ability to create a special idiom for the social setting which he is trying to depict. The most complex experiment in this use of language went into the writing of *No Longer at Ease*. Whereas *Things Fall Apart* and *Arrow of God* are domi-

*For a good example see Lindfors, B., 'The Palm Oil with which Achebe's words are Eaten', *African Literature Today*, No. 1, Heinemann, London, 1968, pp. 3–18.

nated by the poetic, figurative and formal style that is characteristic of traditional conversation and which suits the easy pace and the formalized life style of Umuofia, the urban complexity of *A Man of the People* needs to adopt journalese and cliché to express it adequately. *No Longer at Ease* has to move between the two. Within the city the author tries to capture the speech habits of the colonial officials, educated Nigerians such as Obi, urbanized labourers who have learnt a little English and a whole range of other groups who cannot easily be fitted into any of these categories. In the rural areas there are the Christians who have had to widen the traditional idiom to embrace new areas of experience and there are the other Ibos on whom modern life has had relatively little impact. The complexity of the situation is further complicated by the fact that there are many people who use English, Pidgin and Ibo in varying circumstances. The language in which they choose to express themselves and the way in which they do so reflect their thoughts and their life-style. It is through their language that we are able to enter their world and to share their experiences. As Achebe has said:

> No man can understand another whose language he does not speak (and 'language' here does not mean simply words but a man's entire world view).[5]

Not least among the problems which face the new Nigeria is the fact that verbal communication is no longer as simple and straightforward as in the traditional setting. There are many things which Obi will not attempt to communicate to his parents simply because they do not possess the only language in which he can express his ideas about certain situations. This barrier of communication between the various layers of society has been commented upon by Arthur Ravenscroft:

> While Umuofians pontificate at their meetings in the cliché-ridden English of the popular press and render thanks to 'the man above', they still quote traditional Ibo proverbs at one another. The humblest, the least-educated speak Ibo to fellow Umuofians, otherwise pidgin. The educated speak English of varying degrees of formality, and break into pidgin when they wish to sound friendly. When Obi addresses the UPU after his return from England, he begins in a patriotic burst of Ibo but gradually settles into the English he is more familiar with. The anglicized cabinet minister reverts to pidgin when he feels expansive among a few friends. These carefully recorded language habits contribute much to the sense of flux and uncertainty that Lagos scenes generate.[6]

Even intimate friends such as Obi and Clara have areas of non-communication because of the differences in their education. Obi's favourite pastimes are poetry reading and political discussion. But neither of these things interest Clara. She is more interested in watching film thrillers. She understands the conventions of the thriller much better than Obi who only sits through the sessions to please her.

A detailed examination of the language used at two different meetings in the novel reveals the way in which the author manipulates the language of different groups of people to express their attitudes and values. One such meeting is held by the villagers of Umuofia as a farewell gathering before Obi's departure for England. The very idea of holding a farewell party for the whole village reflects the sense of oneness in the community which is however, slowly being undermined. The villagers are particularly grateful because it has become the custom for people to entertain only those to whom they have sent invitation cards, a selectivity alien to the village community. Moreover Obi is being sent to England through funds raised by the whole community and, at the gathering, everybody feels entitled to advise him and to make demands upon him. The Rev. Ikedi tells Obi:

> 'In times past . . . Umuofia would have required of you to fight in her wars and bring home human heads. But these were days of darkness from which we have been delivered by the blood of the Lamb of God. Today we send you to bring knowledge. Remember that the fear of the Lord is the beginning of wisdom. I have heard of young men from other towns who went to the white man's country, but instead of facing their studies they went after the sweet things of the flesh. Some of them even married white women. . . . A man who does this is lost to his people. He is like rain wasted in the forest.' (p. 9)

The speech shows the extent to which the villagers of Umuofia have adjusted themselves to the new values. The old days of tribal wars when the highest premium was placed on manhood are now looked upon as the 'days of darkness', with its biblical implications of 'a people who walked in darkness'. It is the man of learning who is revered in the new situation. To this extent and to the extent that the Christian religion has been embraced by many Umuofians the villagers have adopted foreign ethics. But they are still anxious to preserve their identity and would therefore regard it as a great betrayal of the community if any one of them married a foreigner. The prayer at the meeting shows how a curious equilibrium is maintained between the traditional and the new religion. Mary, (the name itself is an indication of change), leads the prayer with:

> 'Oh God of Abraham, God of Isaac and God of Jacob . . . the Beginning and the End. Without you we can do nothing. The great river is not big enough for you to wash your hands in. You have the yam and you have the knife; we cannot eat unless you cut us a piece. We are like ants in your sight.' (p. 8)

This is a good example of the way in which the local idiom has been stretched to embrace new concepts, and in which foreign concepts are being reinterpreted to fit into familiar patterns of experience. At the party kegs of palm-wine are laid side by side with plates and spoons which the local parish stocks for the use of its members during public ceremonies like this one. Everything is changing and one of the best ways to observe this change is to listen to the way the people speak and compare it with the way their fathers spoke in *Things Fall Apart*. In the earlier novel no one would have said: '. . . our brother would have become like the king in the Holy Book who called a wedding feast.' (p. 10)

No Longer at Ease is Achebe's first novel to be set in the city and it seems that a deliberate contrast between the city and the country is being projected. Even in the country the author conveys a certain amount of ambivalence in the conflicting cultural attitudes; however the prevalent consciousness is still circumscribed by traditional values. The contending forces resolve themselves into some kind of harmony which is characteristically absent in the city. The tribal solidarity which the villagers bring with them from Umuofia cannot give an adequate sense of security to its members in Lagos. Soon after the beginning of the novel we see a meeting of the Umuofia Progressive Union in Lagos. In the words of the chairman we detect a sense of bewilderment and insecurity: 'We are strangers in this land. If good comes to it may we have our share. . . . But if bad comes let it go to the owners of the land who know what gods should be appeased.' (pp. 5–6). After every sentence the villagers cry *Amen*. There is a greater uncertainty in their behaviour than at the meeting which takes place in the village, where they pray to the Christian God but simultaneously break kola for the ancestors. There is a considerable degree of dissent from members who feel that they should not waste their efforts on Obi who has already defied the Union and asserted his right to regulate his own life. Once again, however, tradition asserts itself and the situation is resolved in the piquant proverb: 'The fox must be chased away first; after that the hen might be warned against wandering into the bush.' We know, however, that this is a formula that does not apply any more. Obi will not come back to them. His downfall is caused mainly by his attempt to live a half-hearted life in a society where he might have been heroically committed to reform, or have survived by accepting to be part of the social corruption. His attempt to satisfy the demands of the community upon him is half-hearted too. He is torn between alternative ways of life but his dilemma does not move us deeply because the author fails to convey any deep human anguish or struggle.

There are occasions however, when the author seems to take local imagery as a substitute for clarity. It is said about Obi for example that 'whenever he ate too much pounded yam he felt like a boa that had swallowed a goat'. (p. 81). The likening of Obi's feelings to those of a boa does not help us to understand them better. On another occasion we are told that 'When the period of guilt was over Obi felt like metal that has passed through fire'. Again the nature of Obi's feelings is not communicated to us in this contrived image. Fortunately this kind of strained and self-conscious description is comparatively rare. Through his keen sensitivity to the way people express themselves and his delicate choice of idiom the author illuminates for us the thoughts and attitudes of the whole range of Nigerian social strata.

Achebe is essentially a moralist. Whether he is handling polemical issues as in *A Man of the People* or is concerned with cultural dilemmas as in his first and third novels, the pivot on which the fictional world revolves is moral concern. As a moralist Achebe tends to paint an uncompromising view of the world. Even in the most ordered society essential human values are constantly being assaulted. In a society where the absence of a strong tradition undermines the emergence of a desired moral order human values are constantly abused. The author rarely obtrudes to state his own views about the situation but dramatizes it so as to disturb the reader's feeling about the direction being taken by society. We are constantly aware that a delicate balance must be preserved between man's material and spiritual pursuits. In the world of *No Longer at Ease* the acquisitive and competitive values of society have been given free rein and have made man lose his sense of justice and self-sacrifice. Ministers admit publicly that they take bribes, taxi-drivers overload their cars and drive at dangerous speeds while they howl insults at each other across the streets and traffic officers take advantage of the situation to extract further bribes. Young girls offer their sex for favours and even doctors grant sick leave for a small fee. In this social imbroglio the individual who seeks to assert his own moral sense finds himself overwhelmed. This is the picture which the author gives of Nigeria during the period of self-government, on the eve of independence. It is the outsider, Mr Green, who voices doubt about the country's future. He tells Obi:

> 'There is no single Nigerian who is prepared to forgo a little privilege in the interests of his country. From your ministers down to your most junior clerk. And you tell me you want to govern yourselves.' (p. 139)

Obi cannot but admit it, although he in turn blames the colonial authorities for having built up the society on the basis of privilege. But whatever excuses Obi might make, he cannot deny that his country is becoming a soulless nation in danger of collapse.

Beti's *Mission to Kala*

Mongo Beti's satire of colonialism is of a much lighter tone than that of Ferdinand Oyono. But the two Camerounian writers share the same basic concern about the illusion of progress which was fostered in Africa during the colonial period. The two writers set out to dispel this illusion by unmasking the ugly face of colonialism.

In *Mission to Kala**, Mongo Beti exposes the negative roles played by missionaries and Western education in Africa. He does this by presenting an adolescent school leaver who has been disoriented by these influences.

Jean-Marie Medza, the hero of the novel, is presented in his critical period of maturing into a man. The progress of his mind towards understanding is presented dramatically as a conflict between different sets of experiences. This conflict leads Medza into questioning all the values which he has taken for granted during his childhood. The end leaves the hero groping for answers which are difficult to find. By leaving the hero in this state of puzzlement the novel avoids complacency. Through this final bewilderment of the hero, Mongo Beti is able to assert that there is no magic key to the treasure-house of experience.

The 'argument' of chapter one sets the mock-heroic tone in which the hero is to tell of his experiences. By adopting this tone about himself the hero-narrator suggests a self-critical attitude about himself. But the tone also implies a degree of cynicism which will not permit him to make an objective appraisal of his circumstances. He will couch his story in understatements and exaggerations so that it will appear to be told from a highly subjective standpoint. He is an unreliable witness.

Medza's stilted view of himself stems from the notion of superiority which he has acquired after his half-exposure to Western education. This makes him highly patronizing to his relatives and fellow villagers and gives him a particularly condescending attitude towards the people of Kala. He is dismissive about every opinion except his own. When he is called upon to go on a mission to retrieve his uncle's wife he complains about being blackmailed by his family into wasting his time. He is critical of his aunt's constant rides to the city, of his father whom he regards as a bully and of the village chief whom he refers to as 'an ancient lecher'.

Nevertheless, in spite of his priggishness, Medza keeps the sympathy of the reader. This he does through his occasional willingness to mock himself the way he does others. From time to time he makes confessions which

*Beti, Mongo, *Mission to Kala*, African Writers Series, Heinemann Educational Books Ltd, London, 1969 (1958).

show that he does not take himself too seriously. This makes clear the fact that Medza's priggishness is merely a mask to hide his confused state of mind. Although he is rebelling against all the moral and social values of his society he is also willing to be frank about his own inability to suggest any superior values. This establishes a tone of intimacy between the narrator and the reader and makes the reader more sympathetic to Medza's plight.

To a certain extent Medza's feeling of superiority towards the village folk is justified. He has lived in his native village of Vimili, spent some years in a boarding school and sojourned in the remote village of Kala. Through these different exposures he has come into contact with varying social conventions, none of which he can now take for granted. He is therefore advantageously placed to comment upon and evaluate the three sets of values. We might therefore be led to expect much from Medza. But he often disappoints us by his failure to be consistently self-critical. He is so impressed by his new-found ability to criticize other people that his comments become marred by his desire to sound wiser than he is. Up to the end he remains an adolescent who is anxious to show off his independence of mind and to claim that the recent discoveries of adolescence have turned him into a sage. His discourse on women, which is but one of his numerous voluble social statements, will serve as an example:

> On the one hand I was amazed at the great discovery I had made, and delighted by its possibilities; but on the other hand I reproached myself bitterly for not having been more daring. Truth to tell, the mere touch of that warm, electric body had given me very real pleasure. At bottom, if I reproached myself for not having pushed matters farther, it was simply because this would, as I supposed, have increased the amount of pleasure I derived from the act. This was a theoretical notion which I afterwards modified: experience has convinced me of this cardinal truth—that the height of pleasure one can reach with a woman stops just short of intercourse itself. This may not be your opinion, but it represents my own sincere belief. I also contend that the best way to stay in love with a woman is never to go to bed with her. (p. 97)

This kind of hollow pontification is made upon a wide range of subjects in which the adolescent school-leaver obviously can lay little claim to having special knowledge. However, from time to time, Medza qualifies these statements with an admission of his limitations. For example after he has been talking at length about geography to the people of Kala he makes the following admission only to slip back into his pretentious moralizing:

> I knew perfectly well that as my knowledge of real Russian life was very vague and sketchy, my only chance of coming through this ordeal unscathed was to invent my own version. The illusory nature of college learning could hardly have been better illustrated, as I learnt for myself

> that night. I was not without a certain pride in all I had learnt during the past academic year: yet at the first real test of my knowledge—a test imposed by genuine circumstance, not under the artificial conditions of an examination-room—I had already discovered vast gaps in the frontiers of my tiny kingdom. (p. 67)

Soon after his arrival in Kala, Medza becomes aware of the great gap between his idea of himself on the one hand and his actions on the other. Although he thinks of himself as a conquistador there is hardly anything he does in Kala on his own initiative. When he is with the young people—all of whom he looks down upon—he finds himself doing anything they suggest. When he is with his uncle or with the chief he fails to resist their patronizing attitude to the extent that he is even coerced into marriage with the chief's daughter because the chief wants him to be his business agent in town.

Medza's only claim to social distinction is his monopoly of Western education in the village. But when the people of Kala make casual inquiries about schools, the superficial nature of his education is exposed. In order to define geography to the people of Kala, Medza has to talk about Russia and New York which to them, as much as to him, can only sound mythical.

It is this experience of having to explain to his own people what Western education is really about that makes Medza begin to question the adequacy of this education. As he awakens to the fact that his 'learning' is made up of textbook clichés he also begins to appreciate the relative adequacy of the experience which the Kala people acquire automatically as part of their upbringing. They seem to be more at ease in their environment and as Medza comes to an increasing realization of this fact his attitude of condescension slowly changes until he finds himself admiring the simple villagers.

> I'd have given all the diplomas in the world to swim like Duckfoot Johnny, or dance like the Boneless Wonder, or have the sexual experience of Petrus Son-of-God, or throw an assegai like Zambo. I wanted desperately to eat, drink, and be happy without having to bother my head about next term, or such depressing things as revision-work and orals. (pp. 58–9)

By the end of his sojourn in Kala his original attitude to the villagers has been completely reversed. He has come to view the rustic simplicity of Kala with envy. This implies, on Medza's part, the acquisition of social and intellectual modesty which he did not possess at the beginning.

The acquisition of modesty enables Medza to begin to question the value and relevance of the school education that he has had and this questioning leads him into rejecting school altogether. He realizes that the school has made him smug and alienated him from his community. His rejection of Eliza, a city girl, is the symbolic turning point. He opts for a village girl in whom he hopes to find the innocence that he associates with rural life.

However, Medza's honeymoon with the village is short-lived. He is appalled by the selfish motives of those who offer to him their friendship. His rejection of Edima is the symbolic end of this honeymoon with Kala.

Once Medza's revolt has begun, it is total. He revolts against all forms of authority, symbolized by his father; he revolts against foreign education, symbolized by school; and he revolts against traditional values, symbolized by Kala. But this rebellion is not altogether rational. His language seems to suggest an adolescent pride in the discovery that even the older generation and the established institutions of society can be criticized. The adolescent rebel seems anxious to show off to the world that he can make independent judgements, even if this implies exaggerating other people's faults. His changed relationship with his father is the best illustration of his pride in rebellion for its own sake:

> I took to keeping a daily journal in which I noted down every detail of my father's behaviour. I set about analysing him as a case-history. I use the words advisedly; as the result of some smattering of psychology which I had picked up at college, I had come to the conclusion that my father would be better off in a psychiatric clinic or even possibly an asylum than in his own home. (p. 172)

This new attitude in Medza represents a change, a change towards maturity. But the same sceptical and flippant tone of the beginning still remains, and this leaves the reader in a certain amount of doubt about how to take Medza's final evaluation of his experiences.

Thus Medza's mission to Kala exercises a profound influence upon his life. It affords him an extra dimension of social experience and leads him to that position of social detachment from which he is able to view everything in perspective.

Up to the time of his departure from Kala his life has been managed for him by someone or other—by his father, teachers, uncles and chiefs. In a way he has been sheltered from responsibility. But at the end of his Kala adventure he finds himself forced into responsibility when the chief coerces him into marriage. With a wife and property he finds his hands tied. He begins to kick against everything and then realizes that the only way out is to become master of himself and take decisions about his own life.

That Medza, in spite of his pretentiousness, retains the sympathy of the reader, depends, among other things, upon the hero's enduring wit, which in turn depends upon his willingness to laugh at himself as much as at others. Through his wit Medza manages to prejudice us against the other characters and we let ourselves laugh with him at everybody else's expense without necessarily accepting everything he says. The reader is in a way flattered by the narrator's willingness to confide in him and share with him his criticism of society's faults.

Mongo Beti's satire is directed above all against the half-baked products of colonial education. Jean-Marie Medza, the confused adolescent who is intoxicated with self-esteem and attracts the undeserved respect of the curious villagers of Kala is an effective caricature of this group of Africans. But in criticizing the narrow-mindedness and perversity of Medza's type, by implication, Beti is criticizing the institutions which have produced such a misfit in society.

Eustace Palmer concludes his discussion on *Mission to Kala*[7] by suggesting that the novel does not attack colonial education or Western civilization. He asserts that the satire is exclusively directed against the 'half-baked' young men who, because of their partial exposure to Western civilization, feel superior to their fellow countrymen. This appears to be a very limited interpretation of the novel. If Medza feels superior to his countrymen it is because superiority has been inculcated in him by the education he has had. Medza cannot take all the blame for the dislocation of social relationships. If the father loses control of the son the father is partly to blame because it is he who sent the son to school, apparently without having made any allowances for the inevitable transformation of the boy's personality.

Nor does Beti spare the traditional institutions of African society. Medza's tirade of criticism is often directed against the selfishness and tyranny of the older generation who seem to see the younger generation as extensions of themselves. The family appears to be a form of institutionalized exploitation of women and children by men. Marriage appears to be more of a social force than a relationship between two human beings. The power of the chiefs is shown to be subject to the worst forms of abuse.

Among the social faults that the novel attacks is the society's acquisition of foreign materialistic values. This does not imply any romanticization of traditional economic relationships. Only the character of the exploitation of man by man changes.

Medza's disillusionment with the values of his society lands him in the painful position of being alienated from his community and its institutions. The pessimistic tone of the epilogue contrasts with the zest for life and enjoyment of adventure which characterized the early part of the novel. At the end life has become meaningless and absurd for Medza and he realizes that this is the inevitable plight of those who get caught in the cross-currents of different civilizations.

Mongo Beti's satire shows confused African communities emerging from social and economic backwardness and embracing values which result in the social disintegration of the communities so that the security provided by the traditional community structure is taken away without any substitute being provided.

That Mongo Beti, in all his novels, adopts satire as his vehicle of social criticism is in itself significant. Satire has tended to flourish in societies which are self-conscious about standards of morals and manners, the reason being that a satirist needs to assume certain values against which he can depict aberrations. The twentieth century is not an age of clearly defined and accepted social values, and this is particularly the case in Africa, a continent which is commonly depicted in contemporary literature as a cesspool of conflicting values. Mongo Beti makes this very lack of established standards the basis of his satire. The twentieth century is not an age in which conformity to conventional values is highly regarded. It is an age in which much greater respect is paid to individual conviction rather than the worship of doctrines and conventions. When we laugh at Medza's use of textbook clichés we are criticizing his lack of originality, his uncritical assimilation of foreign education. The satirist then appeals to our civilized commonsense, to our ability to make rational evaluations of situations rather than holding preconceived notions about the social views of the reader.

Both Beti and Achebe demonstrate through their fiction the alienating influence of foreign education. They show the dilemma of the individual who is cast out of his society because he lives by different standards from those of his community. The idea of progress through 'learning' is criticized. The communities which are portrayed by the two writers are those which have lost the capacity to cater for the social and moral needs of many of their members.

NOTES

1. Ravenscroft, Arthur, *Chinua Achebe*, Longman, London, 1969, p. 20.
2. Achebe, Chinua, *A Man of the People*, African Writers Series, Heinemann Educational Books Ltd, London, 1966.
3. Achebe, Chinua, *Things Fall Apart*, African Writers Series, Heinemann Educational Books Ltd, London, 1962 (1958).
4. Achebe, Chinua, *Arrow of God*, African Writers Series, Heinemann Educational Books Ltd, London, 1965 (1964).
5. Achebe, Chinua, 'Where Angels Fear to Tread', *Nigeria Magazine*, no. 75, Lagos, 1962, p. 62.
6. Ravenscroft, *op. cit.*, p. 19.
7. Palmer, Eustace, *An Introduction to the African Novel*, Heinemann Educational Books, London, 1972.

3. Nationalism

Abrahams' *A Wreath for Udomo*

WHEN nationalist movements all over Africa began to agitate for change history offered a set of dramatic events from which novelists could draw material for interpreting the ever-changing life patterns. The tensions which were generated by the independence movements have been recreated by many novelists, among them South Africa's Peter Abrahams, Nigeria's T. M. Aluko as well as Kenya's James Ngugi. The immediate consequences as well as the wider significance of the fight for freedom have had varied interpretations, but in most instances the support for the nationalist cause expressed in these novels has been qualified by great anxiety about the ultimate achievements of this movement.

Peter Abrahams' *A Wreath for Udomo** which is set in an imaginary African state, Panafrica, sketches the growth of a nationalist movement, first in Europe and later in Africa, up to the time that independence is achieved. The last part of the novel describes the problems of independence and does so with a scepticism which casts doubt on the ability of the new states to maintain political and economic progress. The novel warns that even what has been achieved during the colonial period might be lost in the backlash of traditionalist against progressive forces.

The novel opens with a scene in a pub in the Hampstead area of London. It is here that Udomo first meets Lois Barlow, the English woman whose life is to become unhappily entangled with the African liberation struggle. In the pub, Udomo, poorly dressed and in a lonely, hostile world, is sustained by a sense of defiance against the conditions which hold him down. In his brooding, Lois reads unmistakable self-confidence and depth of mind. During their brief stay in the pub Udomo discovers that Lois knows Thomas Lanwood, the nationalist from Panafrica, who has been writing and agitating for freedom in Britain for nearly a quarter of a century, and this is the man for whom Udomo has been looking impatiently. A

*Abrahams, Peter, *A Wreath for Udomo*, Faber and Faber, London, 1956.

friendship develops between them and Lois introduces Udomo to the circle of nationalists from Panafrica with whom she already has associations. Because of the pattern of colonial education all these young African intellectuals have found themselves together in England from where they launch their united attack. Ironically it is also safer for them to agitate in England where they enjoy a freedom of expression unobtainable in the colonies.

The novel is divided into two parts. The first is called 'The Dream' and covers the period in which Udomo is organizing a Panafrican independence movement from England. There, among friends who share the same ideals and distanced from home by many years in foreign countries, Udomo is moved to a blazing patriotism. But this patriotism is mixed with a curious sentimentality. Some of his thoughts about Africa are highly self-indulgent and sometimes we get the impression that he is being used to express the author's own nostalgia. Udomo describes Africa to Lois in these words:

> 'Africa? She is a little heart. You've seen the shape of her. It's like a heart. Africa is my heart, the heart of all of us who are black. Without her we are nothing; while she is not free we are not men. That is why we must free her or die. That is how it is.' (p. 57)

However, it is clear from what happens later in the novel when Udomo goes back to Africa that his patriotic feelings have an element of unreality. When he faces the facts of political office Africa ceases to be a little heart, or a kindly, tender soothing mother. It becomes an ugly practical problem. In fact when Udomo goes back to Panafrica he can no longer think about Africa in a general and romantic way. He has to think about his own country, and is finally led to betray a fellow nationalist in order to secure the interests of this country which he leads. While Udomo was in London he could not fully comprehend the implications of his commitment, and Lois's love gave him the emotional security which encouraged him to see his ambition as a grand dream. But back in Panafrica even this relationship with Lois turns out to have been transient and illusory, incompatible with the cause to which Udomo is dedicated, his country's freedom.

The organizational problems and personal conflicts of the London days are vividly captured. Although all the participants in the nationalist agitation are committed to the same goal they often fail to present a solid front. For each of them the struggle has a different meaning, even if they do not always realize it. Lanwood, the leader, is a brilliant theoretician but has little to contribute to the practical aspects of the struggle. He has lived in England for so long that he has lost contact with his native country. His writings impress English liberals but the African masses for whom he is pleading cannot understand him. Someone else is needed to act as a bridge between his ideas and the aspirations of the peasants and workers in Africa. It is this role which Udomo and Mhendi fulfil. Lanwood's attitude to freedom is intellectual and he can write about the subject in rhetorical English from a luxury flat in Hampstead, but his distance from the problems about which he has become his country's spokesman is established when he goes back to Panafrica only to find how little contact he has with that society. Mhendi is not exaggerating when he says of Lanwood that 'for him it's an impersonal game of chess. He doesn't really care about people. He hates imperialism impersonally and wants African power impersonally.' (p. 28)

The work of the African nationalists in England is aided by the growth of liberalism in Britain and the growing political consciousness of the oppressed peoples. The British politicians are nervous and want to consult and to a certain extent appease African nationalist leaders. Lanwood speaks with confidence when he tells Udomo: '. . . World forces are moving in our direction. Our friends and allies are getting stronger. Time is with us.' (p. 25). But there is a big difference between the nationalists and their white liberal supporters and this difference constantly manifests itself at Labour Party meetings to which these nationalists are invited. The Africans are rude and discourteous. They interrupt meetings with outbursts of self-righteous anger. It is evident from the meeting which is described in detail that the white liberals are armed with facts and can describe colonial emancipation in a cold, detached and intellectual manner. They appeal to the Africans not to be hysterical and to abstain from using 'shocking' language. But the Africans insist on dwelling on the moral aspects of the debate and assert their right to denounce what they see as the inhumanity of colonialism. Their position is made clear in Lanwood's address to the meeting. He shouts at the liberals:

> 'The one thing you people seem congenitally incapable of understanding is the question of freedom. There is no substitute for it. The colonial peoples are on the march, Mr Chairman, not in the direction of uplift, either economic or moral, but in the direction of freedom, in the direction of determining their own destiny in their own way. We've been accused of being negative and destructive. I'm not ashamed of admitting that it is so. . . . We must be negative and destructive until we are free.' (pp. 74–5)

And earlier when a young liberal peer who comes to Lois's party advises Udomo and Mhendi to:

> 'Be constructive and responsible when you write or speak. Drop Tom Lanwood's violent and irresponsible slogans. You people can help us work out a basis for co-operation. . . .'

Mhendi replies:

> 'It is our business to be irresponsible! A slave's business is to get rid of his chains; not to be reasonable! Only the free can afford to be diplomats.' (p. 36)

For the Africans freedom and self-determination are everything and invalidate all other arguments. They insist that what they are going to do with their independence once they have got it is nobody else's business. This attitude makes co-operation with the liberals very difficult. The liberals want an assurance that Western liberal institutions are going to be preserved in Africa after the various countries have become independent. One of the liberal speakers at the meeting says:

> 'We believe that the practice of government, especially democratic government, is a most difficult practice that needs to be learnt with very great care. It is not enough to hand over power to a few specially selected or particularly vociferous local individuals. Such people, if we were to hand power to them, cannot be called to account by unorganized masses with no tradition of participation in local affairs through trade unions, local government and co-operatives.' (p. 68)

Udomo is not capable of making long, impressive speeches such as those of Lanwood, and is too bitter to use words artfully. His speeches tend to be simply aggressive. For him colonialism means the suffering of his people. Mhendi is the only other person in the novel who comes close to sharing this bitterness. Mhendi has been involved in a violent uprising in which blood was shed, including that of his wife. The two are much closer to the people they lead than are the other members of the group, which is why they make competent editors of *The Liberator*, a newspaper addressed to the ordinary people. They can describe the struggle in terms which the ordinary people understand and not in terms of the universal rights of man, as Lanwood tends to do. When Udomo calls upon his countrymen to oppose the colonial government he does so in the name of better pay and better working conditions and they are quick to understand him.

However, the novel tends to oversimplify the organizational work involved in mobilizing mass support even for such a cause as independence. Obstacles such as the challenge posed by traditional rulers, communication problems due to language differences, and the apathy of peasants are minimized. After six months of a cautious journalistic campaign which does not seem to improve the position of the nationalists, Udomo decides to print a fiery issue of the *Queenstown Post*, which he packs with inciting slogans. Before this issue is printed there has been no evidence of organized support for Udomo's views, yet after it has been printed and the distribution handled by an illiterate market woman with no organization behind her the whole country turns to Udomo's side. This appears unrealistically easy, particularly if judged against the scepticism with which the masses often view the activities of nationalist leaders, the powerful opposition of traditional rulers and the bitter factionalism which tends to accompany the early days of nationalist consciousness.

Udomo's success is however made more plausible by the miscalculations of the colonial administration which immediately throws him into jail and thus turns him into a hero in the eyes of the masses. The administration falls into his trap and gives him a much needed weapon. The declaration of a state of emergency is another wrong move by the administration as it leads to world-wide publicity and thus enhances the importance of Udomo's subsequent trial. The tactless manner in which the newspaper episode is handled is partly due to the governor of the colony, who, having only just arrived, relies on the advice of an insensitive and narrow-minded chief, Smithers. Smithers advises a show of strength to frighten the natives, but this traditional weapon now boomerangs and strikes the colonial administration instead of the nationalists. All the same, the author oversimplifies a potentially complex situation: the nationalist leaders make the right moves while the colonial office makes the wrong ones.

There is some evidence that Peter Abrahams had the Ghanaian situation in mind while he was writing the novel. In 1956 the choice of Ghana must have seemed a logical one to Abrahams. There are overt references in the novel to the first independent black country. When Lanwood arrives in Panafrica for the first time he congratulates the leaders with the words:

> 'The first African revolution to succeed, and a bloodless one. Man! You boys have really done a great job!' (p. 200)

Claude Wauthier has pointed out the close similarity between the events of the novel and the circumstances in which Ghana gained independence. He writes:[1]

> Peter Abrahams' novel caused a considerable stir in the Gold Coast in 1956. Appearing a few months before independence, it looked like a gloomy prediction, since the similarities between Udomo's career and the early career of Nkrumah had not escaped notice. The President of Ghana had indeed been helped by the support of the women of his country, who control the small-scale retail trade as is usual on the West Coast of Africa. He had been influenced by the works of the West Indian, George Padmore, a theoretician of African Nationalism, whom he invited to Accra as his advisor immediately after independence. Padmore recalled the character of Lanwood. Sir Charles Arden-Clarke, governor-general at the time, was a man of liberal ideas, like the governor in the book.

A Ghanaian newspaper also quickly pointed out that 'the link with events in the Gold Coast is clear'.[2]

In drawing attention to evident simplification, it must be pointed out that criticism is not being levelled against the novel for the disparity between its plot and the events which led to the independence of Ghana, but rather for its failure to portray the true nature of the difficulties, the bitternesses, the betrayals and the protracted nature of the struggle through which independence was won by many African countries. The emergence of freedom movements in the colonies did not take the sudden and dramatic form which is suggested by the novel. Opposition to the colonial regime had always existed in one form or another before it was organized into political parties, and the long process by which Ghana achieved nationhood has been examined by several commentators, notably Emmanuel Wallerstein.[3] From the beginning of the century the growing professional class of Africans was making increasing demands for economic equality and for an increased political role within the colonial structure.[4] After 1945, however, there was an organized challenge to the legitimacy of colonialism. Between that time and the time when Ghana achieved internal self-government in 1951, growing nationalist consciousness led to boycotts, riots and other violent forms of internal disagreement. Kwame Nkrumah and his radical followers broke away from the first nationalist organization, the United Gold Coast Convention and soon afterwards a host of other smaller parties emerged. It was not until 1951 when a dyarchy was established under which power was shared by the colonial government and the nationalist party that comparatively peaceful constitutional progress was made towards independence.

In spite of the oversimplified plot, *A Wreath for Udomo* is a prophetic novel in its prediction of the disillusionment that was to follow independence. During moments when he is faced with complex dilemmas, when he has to take painful decisions, Udomo's memory recreates the London days and his happiness with Lois. He is forced to acknowledge that 'winning power is the easiest part', involving as it does friendship and companionship in ideals and aspirations. During the days when he is participating in political agitations in London he draws moral sustenance from the companionship of colleagues and during his few months in prison he takes comfort in the knowledge that the mass of his countrymen is behind him. After independence he finds himself increasingly isolated, surrounded by potential traitors in his own government and party and his political programme held to ransom by external powers which control the economy of the country. He also has to contend with the ambitious rivalries for political office within his own party. As soon as the common enemy, colonialism, is defeated, the people of Panafrica split into factions into none of which Udomo fits. The main cause of factionalism is tribalism, a recurrent theme in the modern African novel, but tribalism is rarely ranked so high on the index of problems facing the new states as it is in this novel. One gets the impression that many writers deliberately side-track the problem because it is too sensitive an issue to be discussed with frankness. For the same reason politicians rarely mention it. They prefer to talk about poverty, ignorance and disease, which do not touch the emotions of the people so immediately. Indeed in recent African writing only Cyprian Ekwensi's *Iska*[5] and James Ngugi's play *The Black Hermit*[6] have treated this problem in significant detail. Because of his personal distance from the setting of his novel Abrahams was able to give this problem a fuller and more dispassionate treatment. Udomo begins to make concessions to the forces of tribalism when he recalls Paul Mabi from London to join the cabinet. Although Udomo knows that Mabi is a sentimental idealist, unfitted for a cabinet appointment, he is compelled to offer him one because it is the only way to get the support of the mountain people. The voters do not choose their candidate on the basis of his policies; ethnic identity is a much more important thing to them.

This recalls Odili's political campaign in *A Man of the People*,[7] when, at the rally which is organized to launch Odili's campaign, the villagers remain apathetic until Max, who is unscrupulous about means, points out that the villagers now have an opportunity to send a man from their own village to where decisions are made. This inspires one of the elders, who gets up and tells his friends:

> The village of Anata has already eaten, now they must make way for us to reach the plate. No man in Urua will give his paper to a stranger when his own son needs it. (p. 125)

The language in which the elder expresses his view emphasizes the idea which recurs again and again in that novel, that as far as the villagers are concerned the nation is a cake to be shared among the constituent sections of which it is made up. In T. M. Aluko's *Chief the Honourable Minister*[8] we again have a situation in which ethnic rivalries play a vital role in the political life of the country. The anti-hero of the novel, Alade Moses, is pushed into the cabinet against his will because it is politically desirable to have a minister from the New Town area of the country.

In *A Wreath for Udomo* tribalism is not presented as merely the rivalry between the various ethnic groups, it mainly connotes strong attachment to tribal customs, which prevents the development of a national consciousness. The tribe and the nation are rivals for the people's loyalty, and disappointingly—for the author—the tribe wins. We are not told to what tribe Udomo belongs, but it is evident that to him this is a matter of little consequence. He is 'detribalized'. He is not only a nationalist, he is also a pan-Africanist. Because of this, independence means something different to him from what it means to his colleagues. Adebhoy and Selina see independence in racial terms and nationalism in tribal terms. Udomo seeks to interpret independence in terms of the economic and social-political transformation of the country in terms of the ideals which he holds for the society, but he is opposed by the forces of tribalism and cultural regression. Adebhoy defends the tribal slant of his nationalism as follows: 'We are a tribal nation, Mabi. Without Selina we couldn't have defeated the Council of Chiefs and Elders.' (p. 242). Udomo himself acknowledges this fact. When Mabi asks him what he is planning to do about tribalism he replies: 'Accept it. It's a fact. If I came out against it today I'd be out of office tomorrow.' (p. 242). Thus Adebhoy submits to the force which he realizes is a great evil to the nation, while Udomo tries to fight it through a gradual process of accommodation. The tribalist faction of the party insists on taking the country back indiscriminately to the tribal ways, which threatens Udomo's efforts to turn Panafrica into a modern state. The difference between him and his supporters becomes unbridgeable, and they assassinate him.

In this novel we see how the problems of a new country intertwine and reduce political policies to ineptitudes. When political canvassing fails to win people away from their tribal loyalties, bribery has to be introduced; and because of the general poverty of the electorate, relatively small amounts of money can play an important role in elections. Thus poverty, ignorance and tribalism work to undermine the creation of a national identity. The manner in which these problems interrelate is partly determined by the personalities of the leaders. Udomo is by far the most important figure in the novel, on whom a great deal depends. A dedicated nationalist and an idealist his chief weakness is his egocentricity. Udomo sees himself as a lone giant fighting against everything that stands in the way of Africa's freedom and progress. The passage which follows not only illustrates Udomo's egocentricity but also conveys the sentimental picture of Africa from which the author cannot be dissociated. On his journey back to Panafrica, Udomo is standing on the deck in the moonlight, waiting for the African coastline to come in view. His expectations are expressed in a sub-biblical language:

> Mother Africa! Oh, Mother Africa, make me strong for the work that I must do. Don't forget me in the many you nurse. I would make you great. I would have the world respect you and your children. I would have the sun of freedom shine over you once more. It was for this I left you for so long and lived in strange lands among strange people and suffered and was abused and was cold and hungry. It was in order to come back to free you, to free all your children, and to make you great among those who now look down on you. They do not understand your dark ways. For them you are something to be exploited and your children creatures to be held down. Now this must end. I will end it if you help me. I cannot see you but I can feel you out there in the dark. Tomorrow I will be with you, in you. Do not let me get lost in your many. Help me, watch me, guide me. My name is Michael Udomo. Do not forget it: Michael Udomo, the instrument of your freedom. . . . (pp. 122–3)

This is but one instance of Udomo's recurrent indulgence in paranoid contemplation. At its worst it shows a lack of control by the author over the character he has created. The reader cannot help being disturbed by Udomo's total lack of modesty which in terms of the structure of the novel appears to be unintentional. This lack of control often causes the sympathies of the reader to diverge from those of the author.

Udomo's insistence on seeing everything as a single sphere with himself at the centre results in his own isolation in the cabinet. He sees all situations as a test of what he stands for. His apprehension of political reality gets twisted so that he begins to see narrow alternatives where they do not exist. The severe choice which he imposes upon himself to betray Mhendi to the neighbouring racist regime of Pluraria is needless and mean. It is not, as Udomo thinks, a sacrifice to the revolution; rather it is a desperate act of a lonely man who has to offer economic success to his country as the only bribe that will keep him in power. Since we cannot sympathize with Udomo in this act of treachery to his principles there is a lack of inevitability in what the author tries to portray as a tragic fall, for the situational imperatives which lead to the fatal decision are not convincing. The crisis could have been averted or at least delayed simply by accepting a less satisfactory amount of aid from another country rather than selling the soul of the nation to the highest financial bidder.

Udomo's tragic stature is left to lean lamely on the strong sense of guilt which he feels after Mhendi's death. His inner urge for expiation makes him confess his treachery to Mabi. Immediately Mabi resigns from the cabinet and a process of recrimination is set in motion until Udomo is assassinated by the orders of his own cabinet and his own party colleagues. Although Udomo says before his death that it is too late to put the clock back we are left with hardly more than a slim hope that the modernization programme which he has started will survive under the leadership of Adebhoy and Selina. In this regard the novel paints a very gloomy picture of the future of the new African states.

The lonely idealist is Peter Abrahams' favourite hero. In his latest novel Abrahams has found a way of saving this hero whose enlightenment is ahead of his time. Josiah, the hero of *This Island Now*[9] saves his own life as well as his revolution by quickly turning himself into a benevolent dictator. Again in this novel the main problem which threatens the revolution is the economic interest of the ex-colonial power and other international monopolies. But because Josiah is endowed with shrewd political tact to back his idealism he uses the poor majority of the country against the vested interest of the minority. Udomo's political weakness partly lies in the fact that he is distanced from the masses. He has to go through tribal representatives to reach the voters. On the other hand Josiah makes a direct appeal to the people. In times of crisis he acts quickly and decisively and only tries to justify his policies when they have already been effectively carried out. When there is need for him to act ruthlessly he does so without any compunction. *This Island Now* is virtually an apology for benevolent dictatorship.

In the passage last quoted attention was drawn to the romantic idealization of Africa and to the apparent inclination of the author to share Udomo's voluble thoughts. The reference to Africa's 'dark ways' may reflect the influence of negritude ideas which were flourishing in the fifties. Besides, Abrahams is trying to create a credible social atmosphere about a part of Africa with which he is unfamiliar. There are echoes of popular stereotypes about the continent. Some of the descriptions of the countryside and reactions of the characters to the environment sound extremely baroque when they are attributed to African characters. Adebhoy's journey through the jungle for example is described in these words:

> Days of gloom and nights of darkness; jungle days and jungle nights. What's the jungle? What's the jungle? And why is it all so green?
>
> Damp earth and no grass
> Dank earth and no air
> Giant trees and dark waters
> Rustle and whisper, hiss and silence
> Stealth and menace
> Is that the jungle?
>
> The jungle is more than trees grown tall as towers; more than darkness, darker than night; more than bog; more than treacherous pool of death; more than giant snake or watchful beast. (p. 220)

This evocation of mystery sounds ludicrously contrived when it is presented as the reaction of a guerrilla fighter such as Mhendi, who would be busy plotting tracks instead of wondering why the jungle is so green. This description contrasts with an effective evocation of mystery which we find in Conrad's *Heart of Darkness** when Marlow is sailing up the Congo river.

> Going up that river was like travelling back to the earliest beginnings of the world, when vegetation rioted on the earth and the big trees were kings. An empty stream, a great silence, an impenetrable forest. The air was warm, thick, heavy, sluggish. There was no joy in the brilliance of sunshine. The long stretches of the waterway ran on, deserted, into the gloom of overshadowed distances. On silvery sandbanks hippos and alligators sunned themselves side by side. The broadening water flowed through a mob of wooded islands; you lost your way on that river as you would in a desert, and butted all day long against shoals, trying to find the channel, till you thought yourself bewitched and cut off forever from everything you had known once—somewhere—far away—in another existence perhaps.

Whereas the vagueness and sense of mystery in the passage from Conrad shows Marlow's hesitancy in making a final assessment of his journey into the unknown, Abrahams' passage sounds like a mystification of the familiar. The description of Mabi's feeling on coming home to Panafrica sounds even more unrealistic:

> Because he was fresh to it, the noises of the little creatures of the night had reached him as a loud chorus behind their talk. Now it invaded their silent room, assumed the proportions of powerful but controlled orchestral music hemming him in on all sides. Up in the mountains, in his home, the young women cut holes in reeds and hung them out so that the wind, passing through the holes, made sweet music. As a boy, a long time ago, he had lain on the grass at night and listened to the sweet solos of the reeds rising above the loud chorus of the creatures of the night. (p. 228)

The description is reminiscent of Camara Laye's *The African Child.*[10] But unlike Camara Laye, who paints an idyllic picture of traditional rural life in Guinea, Abrahams only creates a 'tribal' atmosphere which corresponds to the popular Western view of primitive rites, for example, the description of the 'arranged' marriages of Udomo and Mhendi. But the worst example of a contrived effort to create a 'tribal' atmosphere is the manner in which Udomo's assassination is ritualized. Even African assassinations and *coups d'état* are hardly carried out as dance rituals.

> The man towered above him, knife-hand raised high above his head, body still responding to the urge of the drumbeats, then he brought the knife down and shoved Udomo violently from him. Udomo crashed to the floor.

*Conrad, Joseph, *Three Short Novels*, Bantam Books, New York, 1960, p. 39.

> The drums said:
>
> UDOMO DIE UDOMO DIE UDOMO DIE.
>
> But Udomo still lived. The man at the door had used only his knife handle. But the victim was ready now. The will to resist was ended. The tribal gods had asserted their superiority. Udomo lay on the floor, paralysed, eyes glazed, mouth open.
> And over everything was the throb of the drums, rising now to a mad frenzy.
> The two men, gone mad, whirled about Udomo, leapt over him, played out the ritual dance of death. The drums urged them on.
>
> KILL! KILL! KILL! KILL!
>
> The man who had been at the window shrieked, dipped, and hacked at Udomo's body. (p. 306)

This passage illustrates Abrahams' striving to create a convincing social atmosphere of a traditional African society. The above passage, out of context, could be mistaken for an extract from one of Rider Haggard's novels. The only difference is that Abrahams would claim to be sympathetic to the society which he creates. This however, does not make it any more real. Perhaps more than any other modern African writer, Peter Abrahams writes specifically for a Western audience and in this novel he seems to have made a conscious attempt to create an exotic setting to suit the taste of his audience. But he is also trying to create a 'primitive' society which is in desperate need of 'modernization'. The result is a distortion of an opposite kind from what we find in William Conton's novel, *The African*.[11]

Conton is one of the writers who have tried to recreate the events of transition by an African country from colonial rule to independence. But the author's preoccupation with restating clichés about the purity of the African personality mars the work and compromises its literary qualities. The hero of the novel, Kisimi Kamara, travels to England for further education and finds himself going through a process of disillusionment with the values of the West. Kamara's re-education culminates in a disgust at the discovery that his country 'had been swallowing pills—large and indigestible doses of the materialism of "Western Civilization".' Back home, when he sees the manner in which the people react to violence on the screen of the Western cinema, he affirms what must appear an empty aphorism, that 'the gin of Africa will not mix with the bilge of Hollywood.' This is negritude at its worst, for while the best negritude writers have tried to assert the values of their traditional societies, they have not taken the negative stance of crudely dismissing Western civilization. The narrator of the novel is reduced to the role of a commentator who tries to persuade the reader to see the extraordinary beauty of the African personality. The narrative becomes relatively unimportant. One notes, for example, that Kamara's activity in organizing the nationalist movement for independence is hurried and oversimplified, and when independence has been won everything goes so unbelievably smoothly that the hero feels that he is not needed any more. He departs on a rather grotesque adventure to look for a personal enemy who lives in South Africa. The encounter with the enemy turns into an act of mercy. As Mphahlele has pointed out, this novel 'is a good example of how political slogans, if made a principal of art, can destroy the impact a work of art might have had.'[12] Mphahlele goes on to say that the author of this novel 'is all the time advertising the African way of life to the foreign reader, with an air of discovery. His hero does say he is rediscovering the African in himself. The purity and innocence of Africa . . . naked feet . . . a girl soaping her body and laughing in the rain. The damnable old clichés tht we have come to associate with the colonial or the European who comes to Africa with that back-to-the-womb expression on his face.'

The majority of novels which have explored nationalist themes were written in the post-independence period. Achebe's *No Longer At Ease*, for example, which tries to assess Nigeria's colonial inheritance on the eve of independence, was written four years after the independence of that country. The author is looking back and expressing anxiety in retrospect. *A Wreath for Udomo*, on the other hand, appeared just before the independence of Ghana and before any African country had become independent. This may explain why it seems a less pessimistic novel than Achebe's. But even more importantly, Abrahams tends to show more faith in man's ability to influence the character of his world than Achebe. Achebe would not have created a character like Udomo whose love and sacrifice can save society. The pull of social gravity in Achebe is always too strong for any individual to elevate himself so high. The individual's courage and self-sacrifice are often futile as is the case with Okonkwo in *Things Fall Apart* and with Max Kulamo in *A Man of the People*. Abrahams' heroes on the other hand are often invested with qualities which enable them to attain exemplary goals. In the earlier novels set in South Africa the hero usually asserts that love will triumph against any creed, institution or social system which denies it. In *This Island Now* the hero's vision and courage enable him to change the direction of history and end the oppression of the majority by a minority. In *A Wreath for Udomo* the hero dies after carrying the country across the bridge from the backward past to modern nationhood. He dies in the conviction that what has been achieved cannot be reversed, a view upheld by Paul Mabi in his letter to Lois. By putting this view in the mouths of the two most intelligent characters it is evident that the author intends us to believe that Udomo has started a revolution which is irreversible.

The doubts which both Achebe and Abrahams expressed have been proved by the events of the last decade to have been valid. These novelists have interpreted history for their people and without challenging the idea of independence have warned their societies against complacency as well as thrown light on some of the most controversial issues of our time.

Aluko's *One Man One Matchet*

*One Man One Matchet** stands out as Aluko's most serious novel. The novel centres around the political career of a village rabble-rouser, Benjamin Benjamin, who, inspired by pecuniary as well as social ambitions an recognizing the resentment of foreign rule among the people—especially from the chiefs who have lost much of their traditional power—sets himself up to oppose the colonial administration. But along with these personal motives Benjamin Benjamin also has some vague patriotic sentiments, if not for his country at least for his small village of Ipaja. His intrepidity exposes the weaknesses of colonialism and brings to the surface the underlying conflicts which are inherent in a colonial regime. The conflicting loyalties of the people are heightened and the resulting tensions make the situation so inflammable that violence becomes inevitable. The vulnerability of a colonial system which survives through fear and oppression is thus exposed.

The conflict in the novel is three-fold. The agitator is Benjamin Benjamin who succeeds in enlisting the support of the villagers of Ipaja. He meets with resistance from the colonial administration, which consists of educated Africans as well as expatriates. But within the administration itself there are major differences between the expatriate officers and the educated African administrators. The motives, methods and goals of these different groups are brought into headlong collision in the novel and the author accords them varying degrees of sympathy.

Benjamin Benjamin is a product of the colonial social set-up. He has been dismissed from the elementary school because of a harmless letter he wrote to a schoolgirl. This is due, as Stanfield, the district officer, explains, to the prudishness of the missionary headmaster. But it sets Benjamin off in search of work and he lands a reporter's job on one of the national

*Aluko, T. M., *One Man One Matchet*, African Writers Series, Heinemann Educational Books Ltd, London, 1965 (1964). (Page references are to the reset 1976 edition.)

papers. However, he is not the sort of man to be content to chronicle departures and arrivals in the colonial service. Moreover, his grievance against the system makes him an easy convert for the emerging nationalist party. He starts writing social gossip with a streak of subversion against the system. His lack of experience and his recklessness quickly put him in trouble with the law and he soon lands in prison, but his imprisonment only serves to strengthen his nationalist sentiments. He starts reading a lot of subversive literature on underground activities. We learn that Benjamin himself contributes a 'thesis' on 'The Role of the Chief in the Africa of Tomorrow'.

Benjamin Benjamin is a rogue and a trouble-maker but he attracts our sympathy because he is fighting a system which tries to hold him down and kill the creative power within him. He develops a sharp instinct for self-protection and self-advancement. He quickly grasps the opportunity offered him by the social turbulence caused by incipient nationalism. He plunges into politics, makes laudable speeches about the grievances of his people, which at the same time we know are of secondary importance to his personal interests. His principal reason for joining politics is because it offers him a means of attaining social importance, the conventional path having been denied him through his expulsion from school, and he pursues his goal without any moral scruple. He takes sides with one of the richest men in Ipaja who is also claimant to the stool of Ipaja. All the money which Benjamin gets for advancing this claim ends in his own pocket. Benjamin stirs up strong village sentiments about a piece of land which the colonial administration has taken from them and given to the village of Apeno. It is important for Benjamin, as a self-made politician, to have some visible symbols of social distinction, and he seeks to create this by the way he speaks and dresses. Though in this he bears a resemblance to the European caricatured African of Cary's *Mister Johnson* or Waugh's *Black Mischief** he is a figure noted by African commentators too and is a forerunner of caricatures of West African politicians such as Chief Nanga in *A Man of the People* and Uncle Taiwo in *Jagua Nana*,[13] all of whom look to politics as a means of self-aggrandizement.

Although Benjamin Benjamin no doubt understands that it would be a good thing to cut down diseased cocoa trees, he chooses to oppose the move as a means of winning cheap popularity in the village. He poses as the champion of the people's interests against the cruelties of the Agricultural Department. For the same reason he opposes the tax assessments of the district officer. He is a naturally good performer and quickly becomes accepted as a village leader.

*Cary, J., *Mister Johnson*, Penguin, London, 1962. Waugh; Evelyn, *Black Mischief*, Chapman and Hall, London, 1962.

Because of the hesitancy of the colonial administration to apprehend the agitator there is a gradual deterioration of order which culminates in an outbreak of violence. The administration avoids a confrontation with Benjamin because they know this will turn him into a hero and a martyr. Part of his prestige in the village already depends on the fact that he has been to prison for writing libellous articles against the government. It is during his prison term that he writes his 'thesis' on 'The Role of the Chief in the Africa of Tomorrow'. His friends smuggle reading material to him with the express connivance of the prison warders, a comment on the extent of disloyalty within the government service. The awareness of treachery from within makes the government hesitate to deal with nationalist trouble-makers. This increases the confidence of the trouble-makers, which undermines the prestige of the administration and discredits its effectiveness.

In many respects the confrontation between the colonial administration and the people of Ipaja district is a confrontation between modernity and traditionalism, between progressive forces and reactionary forces. Clearly the sentiments of the author are on the side of progress. In fact traditional institutions are so unfavourably portrayed that the clash appears to be one between efficiency and inefficiency, between organized government and the corrupt, inept, personal authority of traditional rulers. The roughness of the justice which the Oba and his chiefs dispense, the favouritism and arbitrariness with which they discuss the affairs of their district leaves no doubt in the mind of the reader that they are an anachronism and ought to be swept away. The chiefs are prepared to take all the benefits which the administration can offer but are unwilling to co-operate with the government by paying taxes. This evasion of responsibility is a result of sheer ignorance. The richest chief, Alowore, whose original tax assessment is thirty pounds, has it reduced at a stroke to eight pounds simply because he has raised a complaint. The Council takes such measures without any prior inquiry into the state of the complainant's property and in fact there is no system by which such an inquiry can be conducted. The novel is so dismissive about traditional institutions that one cannot help questioning the author's values. His portrayal of an African community is much closer to Joyce Cary's than to any of the modern African novelists. The native chiefs in *Mister Johnson*, like those in Evelyn Waugh's *Black Mischief*, epitomize the stereotyped colonial view of 'native authority' and it would appear that Aluko has adopted this view.

The Ipaja community is shown to be living under a cloak of ignorance and superstition. They will not be convinced that cocoa trees can be sick. Chief Momo will not even believe that mosquitoes carry disease. When

Josia Olaiya, the pastor, tries to explain to him about how mosquitoes transmit diseases he replies:

> 'That is woman talk. Rubbish! Like what that lean White Farmer said about cocoa trees being sick because the trees pass disease to one another—Pastor, the white men that come to us these days do not know their work properly. The good ones have all left our country.' (p. 54)

It is ironical that he should believe in the conquering white man but not in the white man who is trying to help the community by introducing modern techniques. When the local administration decides to start a project to purify water for the village, Momo again dismisses the idea as white man's folly. He finds it difficult to believe that the water which the village has been drinking for so long contains germs. The whole community of Ipaja is presented as ignorant, superstitious and incapable of making intelligent judgements about what is for its own good and what is harmful to its interests. This picture contrasts sharply with villages in Ngugi's *A Grain of Wheat*[14] in which the people have a clear grasp of what is in their interest and are willing to make the highest sacrifices for it, or, for that matter, the village-world of Achebe's novels, where debate and serious consideration are a characteristic feature of village life.

The only good thing which the author says for the traditional community of Ipaja is that the people have a willingness to contribute generously to a common cause in the interest of the community. This is well illustrated by their readiness, sometimes in competition, to subscribe generously to Benjamin Benjamin's numerous funds. First they contribute for the fund set up for claiming back the land which the colonial administration is supposed to have arbitrarily given to the Apenos. Soon after this a tax appeal fund is set up and still they contribute. When Chief Momo is imprisoned they pay towards a Momo Appeal Fund which later automatically turns into a Momo Memorial Fund when the chief dies in prison. If relatively small contributions are made towards this fund it is because the villagers' resources have been taxed to the limit. The poor villagers have also to pay their dues to the church as well as for the education of their children. But their vicarious spirit survives all these demands and collectively they send their most promising children for further education abroad and build community schools for the young ones at home. The novel ends by extolling this quality of the community when the hero, Akpan, says:

> 'To my mind this willingness on the part of the communities to contribute themselves to much-needed services is something that we must preserve in our national character.' (p. 152)

But there is an element of patronage in the writer's attitude and one cannot help thinking that a more sympathetic portrayal of the communities of Ipaja and Apeno would have shown that there was much more than superstition and ignorance to explain their behaviour.

The colonial administrators are presented much more sympathetically than the villagers. Two Englishmen figure as important characters in the novel: Stanfield, the district officer and Gregory, the agricultural officer. Stanfield is a liberal administrator who wants to help Africans and believes that they can be educated to take over the job of running the country, while Gregory is orthodox colonialist who believes in keeping the African in his place. Gregory believes in firmness as the best weapon for dealing with natives and he counsels that Benjamin and all his supporters be locked up, while Stanfield is perceptive enough to realise that such an action would turn the agitators into heroes. However, he has not got a full grasp of the historical forces which are unfolding in the apparently misguided rebellion of illiterate chiefs and their villagers. He still explains events in terms of old clichés such as 'nothing in colonial Africa succeeded at the first time. If it did then Africa would stop being Africa.' He prides himself on knowing the ways of Africa but the way in which he bungles the political crisis shows that his facile opinions about natives are obsolete. While he claims to be a liberal and professes not to share Gregory's scepticism about the capacity of Africans to rule themselves, he demonstrates his own prejudices by the way he patronizes Akpan, the new African administrator who comes to succeed him. He addresses him as 'Udo, my boy' and asks him to think of him as a father. His liberalism goes no deeper than his desire to be identified with the progressive forces—he is particularly anxious to put it on record that he helped an African to take over a position of responsibility.

Whatever differences there are between Gregory and Stanfield, they share a common loyalty to British interests in the colony. This makes it impossible for Akpan, who has the interests of his country at heart, to co-operate with them. Akpan is a much more suitable administrator than they are because he is more interested in the people he serves and also he understands them better. He is the new hope for healing the age-old mistrust. The failure of the colonial administration in operating its social programme is largely due to the fact that the people whom it leads have no faith in it. On its part the government has no confidence in the people: even an educated African administrator cannot be trusted. At one stage Akpan is so frustrated by the mistrust with which he is treated that he hands in his resignation but he later withdraws it because he has to come to the aid of his people in time of crisis. The novel thus indicates that it is from the educated African civil servant that leadership has got to come.

Agitators such as Benjamin Benjamin have their role to play in awakening the consciousness of the people against foreign domination but they are not qualified to give meaningful leadership to the community. The new Akpans have a lot of difficulties to overcome but they are bound to succeed because of their patriotism and devotion to duty. Among the problems which have to be overcome is the cumbersome apparatus of the civil service regulations, clearly unsuited for the African society. Another problem is that of convincing the ordinary people in the village that the educated black man will look after their interests better than the white colonial officer, the people being more inclined to trust their traditional rulers both black and white, even though in the novel, they are shown to be useless.

Through his clear understanding of the situation and his willingness to devote himself to his duty—which sometimes means working for long hours into the night—Akpan is eventually able to gain control of the situation and to demonstrate to the people of Ipaja that the leader whom they have been following, Benjamin Benjamin, has been exploiting them instead of serving their interests. But it is too late to avert violence completely. Akpan might have restored order long before the community was precipitated into the tragic events involving loss of life and destruction of property, but his efforts are undermined by loopholes in the civil service regulations and legal processes which astute trouble-makers such as Benjamin Benjamin make use of.

T. M. Aluko's favourite hero is the well-educated civil servant. In *Kinsman and Foreman*[15] a professional engineer is obstructed in his duties by the unreasonable demands of his kinsmen who require him to assist them by corrupting the public service. Titus Oti refuses to give way to these demands and in the end his integrity triumphs. In *Chief the Honourable Minister* the corrupt and inefficient politicians lead the government into chaos and violence. Finally the only surviving element of stability is the civil service. The top executives of the civil service always remain unblemished. Corruption exists in the lower ranks but the executive class is obstructed from stamping out this corruption by the paraphernalia of orders and regulations which exist at the expense of efficiency. In *One Man One Matchet* the bureaucratic procedures and hierarchical structure of the civil service prevent Akpan from taking the quick action which could have forestalled the outbreak of violence in the district of Ipaja. Before he can act he is required to write long minutes stating his assessment of the situation when he is sure that no one will read through them. He also has to exchange frequent but useless correspondence with the people of Ipaja. He himself is powerless to deal with the tax crisis until the resident officer decides to hold up the salaries of the local chiefs until they have paid their share of government taxes. Before Akpan has had time to congratulate himself he discovers that court charges have been brought against him by the villagers. When he sets up a commission of inquiry to investigate Benjamin's fund-raising activities the chief refuses to co-operate in giving evidence. He seeks the advice of the legal department to determine whether there is sufficient ground for instituting legal proceedings against the trouble-makers but it takes a long time before he can get an answer. When finally the trial does start it is dragged out by legal technicalities only to end in the dismissal of the case because charges were brought under the wrong section of the law. This is interpreted by the villagers as a great triumph by Benjamin Benjamin and Akpan's prestige is greatly diminished. The confidence gained from the case against the government spurs Benjamin to new heights of intrepidity. He incites the villagers into acts of violence and riots break out. Again Akpan's efforts to bring the culprit to face the law are frustrated by bureaucratic complications. Luckily enough for Akpan the excesses of Benjamin's activities turn against him and he is killed by his own supporters.

After all the difficulties that Akpan has to go through in Ipaja, he comes to the conclusion that new regulations procedures ought to be designed for the country. The indiscriminate transfer of rules which have been designed for a different social set-up, makes effective administration very difficult. For instance, in a place where there is a grave shortage of doctors it seems to be a great waste of the doctor's valuable time to examine dead bodies when he should be saving the living. Moreover, in Ipaja the practice of conducting post-mortems is futile because it does not give the necessary certainty to the community about the cause of death. As far as the villagers are concerned post-mortems are some kind of witchcraft practised by Europeans.

The author seems to regard freedom of speech as an unnecessary luxury in a poor and backward community. Udo Akpan, the hero who often voices the opinions of the author says:

> '.... Benjamin Benjamin in Hyde Park would be a most interesting fellow. No one would take him seriously. No more seriously than they take a clown at the Circus. His black face would be a source of amusement to a good number of ice-cream eating Yorkshire housewives holidaying down in London. . . . He would be completely harmless in the London context. . . . But it is an entirely different thing in this country where the masses, illiterate and ignorant, believe everything that anyone that can read and write tells them.' (pp. 150–1)

In other words Aluko is criticizing the indiscriminate transfer of political and social practices from Britain to African communities where very different social circumstances obtain. His own view would seem to be that the masses need to be educated first before democratic freedoms can be extended to them. The colonial administration, however, inadvertently imposes all its values. The attitude of the administration on the matter is expressed by Stanfield, the outgoing district officer of Ipaja. He says to Gregory:

> 'Parliamentary democracy ... is the one great contribution that our country has made to civilization. It is for this that Britain will be remembered long after our empire has passed away.' (p. 8)

Although Aluko credits colonialism with a great deal of benevolence and shows how the ignorant villagers are constantly frustrating colonial officials trying to carry through useful social programmes, he points out that the best service to the African community can only come from educated Africans whose principal loyalty is to that community. The expatriate official puts the interests of his own country first. When he tries to serve the colonial people there is a clash of loyalties. This clash of loyalties is well illustrated by the manner in which Stanfield handles the information about the cocoa crisis. All publicity is geared towards upholding the good name of Britain, which makes it necessary sometimes to conceal important information from Akpan who is himself an agent of government policy.

Tribal hostilities are presented as one of the principal obstacles to progress. The arbitrary colonial boundaries only serve to aggravate the problem. The colonial administration ignores age-old hostilities when it decides to join Ipaja and Apeno into one administrative unit. This gives rise to fierce tensions within the community, which are aggravated by a standing land dispute. Tribal prejudices and antipathies frequently manifest themselves in the activities of the people of Ipaja. At a local meeting in the village one of the chiefs declares to the crowd that the people of Apeno are a breed of vagabonds and thieves, that the first Apeno was a thief and that it was because of this that he was driven away from the palace of the founder of the major dynasty of the tribe and banished to Apeno. Akpan's reception in Ipaja is very cold partly because he comes from a different tribe. He is regarded as a foreigner in the district. In fact when the people of Ipaja talk of their descendants 'both at home and abroad' they are trying to include all members of their tribe who are working in different areas of the country. The tribal associations in the capital recall those in Achebe's *No Longer At Ease*, but Aluko handles the issue much more flippantly by emphasizing its comic aspects. However, the basic problem is posed: How can the new nations of Africa cope with the conflicting loyalties of the different tribal groups? The city, which is the symbol of the new national identity, is often an amalgam of distinct tribal groups which resist integration. The Ipaja dwellers in the novel, wherever they are, always identify with the tribal disputes in their district. Those who live in the capital regularly send money for the various funds which are set up by Benjamin Benjamin to fight dubious causes. In order to attend a rally in Ipaja one of the workers in the capital procures sick leave under false pretences, his loyalty to the national institution where he works ranking below his loyalty to the tribe.

One Man One Matchet evokes the social tensions of the West African social scene when the nationalist movements were beginning to have an impact on the people. The people awaken to the political power which they possess when they are organized. They begin by dissipating this power in their unco-ordinated rebellion against the colonial administration. They obstruct social programmes which are designed for their benefit. Politics get mixed up with social services and in the confusion a self-seeker is mistaken for a true leader. The British administration, which is beginning to lose confidence in its mission, is slow to act and this leads to the explosion of latent tensions which have hitherto been contained by an authoritarian administration. The situation is only eased by the arrival of an educated African administrator.

Not all the educated Africans in the novel, however, behave as responsibly as Akpan. Some of them exploit the ignorance of the people to line their pockets. Lawyers and surveyors take advantage of the Igbodudu land case to enrich themselves. Akpan's investigations of the case reveal that lawyers have charged altogether about four thousand two hundred pounds to plead a case for land worth under two thousand pounds. One surveyor has also benefited unfairly from the case. People like Benjamin Benjamin who have had a little education are the worst enemies of the people's interests. This leaves the well-educated and the experienced civil servant as the only hope for the community. He is the only man who has sufficient integrity to render selfless service to the community. It is from this standpoint that the novel defends the civil servant's participation in politics. The final scene in the novel is a record of a discussion between top civil servants who are reviewing the problems of the country. They all agree (and this itself indicates the degree of complacency in Aluko's view) that they are the best leaders. Udo Akpan says:

> The best brains of the country are with a few exceptions all in the Civil Service. Can this country with its limited resources in educated man-power afford to have their mouths padlocked in the Civil Service while second-rate and sometimes semi-literate men are saddled with the very important duty of legislating and taking executive decisions for the State? Can we not have a state of affairs where the civil servant can make

his views known publicly on matters on which he is by qualification and experience competent to express views? (p. 149)

One Man One Matchet was written in 1964, a few years after Nigeria's independence. In it the author looks back to the period when Africans were beginning to assert their right to govern themselves. In his opinion the class of Africans which was best suited to lead the country was the group of educated Africans who had gained administrative experience during the colonial period. Aluko's politics are reactionary and authoritarian. He advocates some kind of dictatorship by the highly educated Africans. He hardly concerns himself with ideas and policies: his pre-occupation is with civil service regulations and procedures. He writes as a member of the establishment and suggests no radical transformation of this colonial establishment. All he wishes to see is a few men of integrity stepping into the shoes of the colonial administrators.

NOTES

1. Wauthier, Claude, *The Literature and Thought of Modern Africa*, London, Pall Mall Press, 1966, pp. 158–9.
2. *Ibid.*
3. Wallerstein, E., *The Road to Independence*, La Haye, Mouton, 1964.
4. See the writings of W. R. B. Attoh Ahuma, J. Casely Hayford and other members of the Gold Coast Aborigines Society.
5. Ekwensi, C., *Iska*, Hutchinson, London, 1966.
6. Ngugi, J., *The Black Hermit*, African Writers Series, Heinemann Educational Books Ltd, London, 1968.
7. Achebe, Chinua, *A Man of the People*, African Writers Series, Heinemann Educational Books Ltd, London, 1966.
8. Aluko, T. M., *Chief the Honourable Minister*, African Writers Series, Heinemann Educational Books Ltd, London, 1970.
9. Abrahams, Peter, *This Island Now*, Faber, London, 1966.
10. Laye, Camara, *The African Child*, Collins, London, 1959.
11. Conton, W., *The African*, African Writers Series, Heinemann Educational Books Ltd, London, 1964 (1960).
12. Mphahlele, E., *The African Image*, Faber and Faber, London, 1962, pp. 22–3.
13. Ekwensi, Cyprian, *Jagua Nana*, African Writers Series, Heinemann Educational Books Ltd, London, 1975 (1961).
14. Ngugi, James, *A Grain of Wheat*, African Writers Series, Heinemann Educational Books Ltd, London, 1968 (1967).
15. Aluko, T. M., *Kinsman and Foreman*, African Writers Series, Heinemann Educational Books Ltd, London, 1967 (1966).

4. Disenchantment

Soyinka's *The Interpreters* and Achebe's *A Man of the People*

THE attainment of independence by many African countries in the last decade and the resultant change in the social-political atmosphere of these countries has had discernible influence on fictional themes. It has removed, or at least distanced, the common enemy, colonialism, which has been the object of frequent attack, and has made clearer the limited validity of eulogies of the past. A new type of novel which seeks to interpret the present in terms of the human characteristics of an African community without reference to the past has emerged. The present has brought new problems which cannot simply be explained in terms of an external enemy and from which it is impossible to escape by the creation of a romantic or heroic past. As Achebe has written:

> Most of Africa is today politically free; there are thirty-six independent African states managing their own affairs—sometimes very badly. A new situation has thus arisen. One of the writer's main functions has always been to expose and attack injustice. Should we keep at the old theme of racial injustice (sore as it is still) when new injustices have sprouted all around us? I think not.[1]

Achebe is one of the novelists to offer sharp insights into the problems and dilemmas of the new political order in Africa. Another leading writer who has tried to interpret the same situation is Wole Soyinka. In his first novel *The Interpreters,** he captures vividly the decadence and sterility of the contemporary social and political set-up in many African countries.

Soyinka's *The Interpreters* is less overtly political than the majority of novels which have tried to interpret the post-independence dilemmas. None of the characters is a member of the government, there are no Parliamentary debates, no mass rallies, and no cabinet meetings such as we find in *A Man of the People.*[2] The main characters are a group of young

*Soyinka, Wole, *The Interpreters*, African Writers Series, Heinemann Educational Books Ltd, London, 1970 (1965).

intellectuals who are alive to the social realities of their country. They dislike their situation intensely and wish to change it but they find themselves excluded from all positions of influence. They make many varied efforts both individually and collectively to come to terms with the business of living. Partly because they are barred from power by vested interests and partly because they are reluctant to soil themselves by participation in the corrupt system which they abhor, they find themselves drifting outside the main current of events.

The principal characters to whom the title refers are Kola, a painter, Sekoni, an engineer and sculptor, Sagoe, a journalist, Egbo, a Foreign Office official, and Bandele, a university lecturer in art. They are united by youthful energy, intellectual vigour and a cynical disapproval of the moral emptiness of their society. They also share a common interest in art and a desire to change the world around them. Through different media they all seek the power to transform. Kola uses the canvas, Sagoe the newspaper and Bandele the teaching profession. Egbo seeks to dominate men and to use them as material to model the kind of world he would like to live in—although he is evidently uncertain about what kind of world he wants to create. Sekoni is a scientist who wants to change the world through technology, but is frustrated by vested interests. He turns to carving and achieves self-realization by creating a masterpiece, 'The Wrestler', which Kola refers to as 'one of those once-in-a-life co-ordinations of experience and record'. But this kind of achievement has its limitations. In a way it is escapist. Art becomes a consolation and the act of creating compensates the artist's frustrated desire to change the world: he creates his own world, which he has power to order. But the other 'interpreters', who cannot express themselves through art, find ways to associate themselves with Kola's Pantheon, since it expresses their anxieties and enables them to attain an understanding of their social situation and their destinies, and become reconciled to their human limitations.

The novel begins with a scene in a public bar where the interpreters are amusing themselves after a rather half-hearted attempt on a canoe expedition to find Egbo's ageing grandfather, a chief to whom Egbo is a likely heir. Through the conversation of the group we learn that Egbo is faced with the dilemma of succeeding his grandfather or staying in the Foreign Office. He cannot make up his mind which of the two positions would offer him greater scope for exercising power. In any case Egbo seems to be the kind of person who enjoys dilemmas and mysteries about which he can debate aloud, even to the embarrassment of his friends. One thing we learn from Egbo's loud talk is that his grandfather controls a number of smuggling routes and that the government only gets the old man's left-overs. So we learn that the central government is not strong enough to control the traditional chiefs, who are as corrupt as the national leaders. Egbo, who has no moral pretentions also admits that he is attracted to chieftaincy because it will enable him to have a harem of women. During the canoe trip, when the tide changes, Egbo suggests that they turn and go 'with the tide'. The phrase has clearly satirical overtones which Kola catches immediately and says 'like apostates'. The word apostacy has already been used by Kola to describe the failure of the 'interpreters' to translate their desire for change into positive action. Egbo resents this situation more than anyone else partly because he loves power more than anyone else; and perhaps also partly because as a civil servant he leads a more restricted life than the others. But as he informs them, they are all part of the system.

The kind of language which Egbo uses to describe politicians shows his contempt for them. He wants to be liberated from 'bearing the burdens of fools' (p. 13). Later, during the same conversation he says that Sagoe looks as blank 'as a politician at a press conference.' This contempt for politicians is shared by the rest of the group. Sagoe sees his interviewers on the board of *The Independent Viewpoint* as a bunch of 'illiterate, unctuous, aggravating toads'. The superior airs which Sagoe adopts at the interview and the confrontation between him and the members of the board brings into focus one of the main issues which underlie the social conflict described by the novel, namely the antagonism between the intellectual élite and the political élite. As many recent commentators have pointed out, the political élite in Africa today consists largely of professional politicians who, mainly because of their slight education, are not equipped to find alternative jobs. Their main qualification for holding political office is their unquestioning loyalty to the ruling party and to the leader and they are anxious to ensure themselves against opponents who might deprive them of their status.[3] This is the class of people responsible for intolerance, electoral fraud, detention laws and the creation of politically meaningless party systems. Politics has become one of the important openings to social prestige and wealth and the people who acquire status through this channel find themselves in opposition with another group who got it by way of a different channel: education. As Emmanuel Wallerstein has written:

> The two roads to social mobility, the two paths to social prestige—education and politics—are in conflict. This conflict is the nexus around which current political disputes tend to resolve. . . the intellectuals tend to be alienated from the nationalist movement. There is an inverse correlation between education and support for the nationalist majority party . . .[4]

This conclusion was based on research findings in Ghana and the Ivory

Coast. C. P. Lloyd, a sociologist who worked in a wide area of West Africa, has expressed the fear that competition within the élite and conflict with the masses might lead to hostilities which could halt the modernizing process.[5] This same anxiety is expressed, perhaps with graver apprehensions in both *The Interpreters* and in *A Man of the People.*

When Sagoe arrives for his interview by the board of *The Independent Viewpoint* he is already prejudiced against the board members. He knows they will be 'compensation members' who have lost in politics but who have served the ruling party loyally. A wide range of activities in which they might have participated, such as 'Lost elections, missed nominations, thug recruitment, financial backing, Ministerial in-lawfulness, Ministerial poncing, general arse-licking, Ministerial concubinage. . . .' (p. 77)—these are the things which occur to Sagoe as he is going into the boardroom. At first the board members are polite but Sagoe's superior manner provokes them. When the chairman asks Sagoe whether he is an intelligent man the latter replies: 'That depends in whose company I am, sir.' Sagoe makes it clear to the board that he would think it presumptuous of them to try to engage him in any challenging discussion, and informs them that he has not come to beg for the job. The hot exchanges which follow end in Sagoe leaving the room and the Chairman remarking: 'These small fries, they all think they are popularly in demand, just because they have a degree. . . .' (p. 79). The fact that Sagoe is employed in the long run shows that his knowledge is needed and that the people who control the paper cannot do without people like him. But the scene also shows that he is likely to be dependent on the people who wield power. He is only able to assert a mock independence by refusing to recite the expected formal aphorisms to the interviewing board. But he soon learns that if he wants to earn money in journalism he has got to see it as a business and only do what is profitable for his employers.

In *A Man of the People,** Chief Nanga's quarrel with Jalio is an even more dramatic confrontation between a politician and a representative of the intellectual élite, this time an artist. Mr Nanga, the Minister of Culture, comes to open the country's first book exhibition of works by local authors. Although Jalio is his country's most famous novelist, Nanga has never heard of his name, let alone read his books. Nanga rebukes the writer for not dressing according to protocol. Jalio makes it clear through his superior airs that he does not care what the Minister thinks. He states that

*Achebe, Chinua, *A Man of the People,* African Writers Series, Heinemann Educational Books Ltd, London, 1966. (Page references are to the reset 1975 edition.)

he dresses to please himself. Nanga only shows any respect for Jalio when he notices the deferential treatment accorded him by foreign diplomats. This clash between Chief Nanga and Jalio is a clash between representatives of two life-styles, two cultures, each having little respect for the other but each harbouring a secret envy for the other's position in society, a theme used by many recent African novelists. The clash between élite groups in society and their conflict with the masses is often seen as a major cause of Africa's present problems.

In *A Man of the People* the political crisis is triggered off by the expulsion of two-thirds of the cabinet, all of whom happen to be graduates. This is because this group, under the leadership of the Minister of Finance who has a Ph.D. in Public Finance, has set the interests of the nation higher than those of the party. The *Daily Chronicle*, the official organ of the ruling party, gives the following coverage to the incident:

> Let us now and for all time extract from our body-politic as a dentist extracts a stinking tooth all those decadent stooges versed in text-book economics and aping the white man's mannerisms and way of speaking. We are proud to be Africans. Our true leaders are not those intoxicated with their Oxford, Cambridge or Harvard degrees but those who speak the language of the people. Away with the damnable and expensive university education which only alienates an African from his rich and ancient culture and puts him above his people. . . . (p. 4)

As a result of this expulsion of the only people competent to deal with the financial crisis of the country, the situation gets worse and worse. A new group of socialist intellectuals under the leadership of Max challenges the government and publishes facts which bring it into public disrepute; and so the situation gives rise to widespread civil disorder which gives the military élite an opportunity to take over power.

At the end of the novel the army has restored temporary order, but the power conflict is still unresolved and we are only left with a dim prospect of proper order being restored. All the same, there is some hope. In spite of the problems which remain unsolved, at the end we feel that the unco-ordinated national reaction against the excesses of Nanga's regime will at least act as a precedent to restrain similar excesses in the future. After all, the changes which take place are not simply a result of chaotic forces. The collapse of the Nanga regime is the result of a conscious effort by a group of socialist intellectuals, led by Max, concerned about the plight of their country and prepared to organize themselves in order to change the power structure. They are the only group that holds promise for the country because unlike everybody else they are under no illusions. They know what they want and they go about it without any scruples. Max knows from the very beginning that they cannot hope to win the election. The odds are too heavy against them. Max explains to Odili that the plan is 'to get something going and then wait for the blow up'. And the blow up does come. However, the death of Max leaves us in doubt as to whether there will be anyone else to carry on his work. The only thing that Odili plans to do is to found a school in Max's name. But we know that Odili is penniless—except for the limited party funds which are in his possession and which he is already planning to use to pay for his bride.

Thus the end leaves us with a big dilemma and only a little flicker of hope: at least a new patriotic element has begun to emerge within the society, but the future is uncertain. Nor is this ambiguity new in Achebe. In *Things Fall Apart* we are presented with a conflict between two cultures but the end does not leave us with any certainty about whether or not the Ibo traditions are going to survive the invasion of Western values. This type of ambiguity reflects the author's conception of the nature of tragedy. In a clearly intrusive comment through the mouth of Obi Okonkwo in *No Longer At Ease* he states:

> 'Real tragedy is never resolved. It goes on hopelessly for ever. Conventional tragedy is too easy. The hero dies and we feel the purging of emotions. A real tragedy takes place in a corner. . . . the rest of the world is unaware of it.' (p. 36)

The main limitation of *A Man of the People* is that we are only allowed to see the events of the story through the eyes of the narrator—an adolescent, self-deceiving, self-indulgent and naive anti-hero. Odili's comments never rise above naive speculations which are often loaded with clichés. His interpretation of events is too limited to satisfy the interest of the reader. For example when Chief Nanga praises himself openly in public and declares that his motto is, 'Do the right and shame the devil', Odili adds this comment for the reader:

> Somehow I found myself admiring this man for his lack of modesty. For what is modesty but inverted pride? We all think we are first-class people. Modesty forbids us from saying so ourselves though, presumably, not from wanting to hear it from others. Perhaps it was their impatience with this kind of hypocrisy that made men like Nanga successful politicians while starry-eyed idealists strove vaingloriously to bring into politics niceties and delicate refinements that belonged elsewhere. (p. 11)

This kind of comment tells us more about Odili's own immaturity than about the situation which he is trying to describe. We keep suspecting the voice of the author but we are never certain. One gets the impression that the author is hiding behind the narrator to escape from having to make an evaluation himself. In his novels about the past Achebe is able to express a coherent view of life, perhaps because then he can see events in perspective. He seems to have found it more difficult—and understandably so—to shape topical issues into a coherent pattern.

The treatment of the intellectual class in many African novels often reveals an underlying assumption that it is their historic mission to rule their fellow countrymen. If power is wielded by some other group it may be because that group has usurped power which it is misusing, as in *A Man of the People*, or it may be because the more enlightened class, that of the intellectuals, has abdicated from its responsibility, as in *Return to the Shadows*[6] by Robert Serumaga. Sometimes it is a mixture of both, as in *The Interpreters*. But in all three cases the novelist asserts that ultimately it is the intellectual élite which can rescue these countries from the political and social crises by which they are bedevilled.

Nowhere in the African novel is the position of a small westernized intellectual group in a traditional society treated with a deeper understanding than in the Egyptian novel, *Beer in the Snooker Club* by Waguih Ghali.[7] This is a satirical portrait of Egyptian society but done with great love and compassion. The upper class members of 'the club' moving around the swimming pool like a soft breeze, middle-aged men playing croquet, middle-aged women seducing adolescent boys, the docile labourers who attribute everything to the will of God, and the rich gamblers—all united by the sly Egyptian humour and involved in the same tragedy of a society where men die young and houses are crowded with orphans and widows. In this situation, where the upper class is narrow-minded and the working class resigned to what they call the will of God, the small group of westernized intellectuals chase unrealizable dreams and pass lofty judgements based on foreign ethical notions that have nothing to do with the social reality of Egypt. The economy is not wide enough to absorb all these young people and their frustrations drive them into plotting subversion. In turn the government has to adopt repressive measures to protect itself and a vicious circle develops.

Although the social situation which is described in this novel is different from that which obtains in any of the Black African countries, the dilemma of the intellectual who tries to adjust his Western values to a traditional society has parallels in Black Africa. The main characters of Ghali's novel, Font, Ram and Edna, have all been educated in British universities. But even before they left for Britain they grew up in Egypt reading English Literature at a private English school for the children of the upper class. They go to England so that they can come into contact with the life which they have grown to love and admire through their reading. Although their experience in England is disillusioning, it is too late to reject the Western culture which has become part of them. They find themselves condemning everything Egyptian which fails to satisfy the standards they have acquired from their Western education. They get involved in political action which is doomed from the start because they argue about politics as if they were living in England. Only Ram realises the absurdity of their situation. At times he is able to stand outside himself and laugh at it all. But even his intense self-awareness becomes a source of pain because in addition to being haunted by the spectre of man's suffering in general he is haunted by the spectre of his own personal tragedy. His means of escape is women and drink. In the end he attains some kind of uneasy truce with the world and himself by surrendering himself to physical passion and seeking comfort in a marriage with a rich woman.

There is a close resemblance between Ram's situation and that of several of the characters in *The Interpreters*, notably Sekoni. Like Ram and Font, the young intellectuals in *The Interpreters* are impatient with the morbidity of their society. They dislike the way their country is being run and are determined to change the situation and shape it according to their own ideals, but they soon discover their limitations as individuals. Sekoni goes through the bitterest experience of all. A qualified engineer, soon after his return from his studies abroad he is offered an office job which involves spending most of his time in the daily performance of small administrative duties such as approving bicycle advances for clerks, sorting out application forms for clerical posts and attending committee meetings. He protests to his boss and this leads to his being exiled upcountry where, he is told, 'you may work with your hands until your back blisters'. On his arrival in the little village of Ijioha, Sekoni builds an experimental power station, but his boss has invested in a power-supply monopoly, so an expatriate is hired to condemn the experimental station. When Sekoni tries to test it himself he is arrested and forcibly taken to a mental hospital. As soon as he is free he begins to carve a figure which he calls 'The Wrestler'. Although the figure of the carving resembles that of Bandele, the subject has unmistakable identity with Sekoni's own life. The 'balance of strangulation before release' expresses the sculptor's own frustrations. It is also significant that he dresses the figure in a pilgrim's dress. The pilgrimage may refer to the interpreters' quest for moral and political order, but also to the larger pilgrimage of man's life.

After Sekoni has achieved, in a single masterpiece, an understanding of himself and his place in the world, he has little to do in the novel until he dies in a motor accident. The description of his death brings home to the reader that this novel is a poet's novel:

> The rains of May become in July slit arteries of the sacrificial bull, a million bleeding punctures of the sky-bull hidden in convulsive cloud humps, black, overfed for this one event, nourished on horizon tops of endless choice grazing, distant beyond giraffe reach. Some competition there is below, as bridges yield right of way to lorries packed to the running-board, and the wet tar spins mirages of unspeed-limits to heroic cars and their cargoes find a haven below the precipice. The blood of earth dwellers mingles with blanched streams of the mocking bull, and flows into currents eternally below earth. The Dome cracked above Sekoni's short-sighted head one messy night. Too late he saw the insanity of a lorry parked right in his path, a swerve turned into a skid and cruel arabesques of tyres. A futile heap of metal, and Sekoni's body lay surprised across the open door, showers of laminated glass around him, his beard one fastness of blood and wet earth. (p. 155)

The passage is a powerful evocation of a wild storm. Sekoni's death is only mentioned in the last sentence, and we are made more aware of the cosmic menace than of the snapping of a man's life. Sekoni's dead body in the small heap of metal and blood is insignificant in the raging storm. The passage is laden with the imagery of the natural processes of creation, growth and death—all in one wild confusion where man intrudes almost accidentally.

The incident marks a turning point in the thematic progression of the novel. Coming at the beginning of the second part it links the world of politics and the world of art. Whereas the first part portrays the interpreters' attempt to define their lives in political terms, the second part is concerned with their attempt to define their role in the continuity of life, mainly through art. The death of Sekoni brings to them a painful awareness of their limitations and their mortality. Their youthful vigour becomes dulled by painful contemplation. Egbo runs away and hides among rocks until the funeral is over; Sagoe locks himself up in a room full of beer and vomit, while Kola seeks escape in his painting. The group meets again after two weeks, still sad and bewildered and they never recapture their liveliness again. The moral decay of this world equals the physical decay which surrounds them. However, unlike everybody else, they have a place to escape from the squalor of the world around them. This is paralleled by the presence of one clean toilet room for the senior staff; the rest have to use a room covered with excreta.

Efficiency is impossible when things are run by men like Chief Winsala who can make such boasts as 'In the morning I drink whisky, in the evenings I drink schnapps. In the afternoons I don't drink at all, I sleep . . .' (p. 83). Another set of people of the calibre of Nwabuzor, have to be found to maintain some kind of order in the system. He is the editor of *The Independent Viewpoint* and when Sagoe threatens to resign over the suppression of the article on Sekoni, Nwabuzor tells him:

> 'Sagoe, look, I have been in this game for thirty years. Believe me there was a time when I held these ideals. I moved from one paper to the other, leaving in a flurry of rightcous indignation. But look man, journalism here is just a business like any other. You do what your employer tells you. Believe me, Sagoe, just take my word.' (p. 95)

It is men like Nwabuzor who have sold their souls for money that keep the system going. Lasunwon belongs to the same category of educated people who have decided that only money and their physical comfort matters, that in the end you'll find it's every man for himself.

The academics are satirized as much as the politicians. Characteristic representatives of this class are Dr Faseyi and Professor Oguazor. The former, who is married to an English wife, is always rebuking her for not behaving like an English lady. At an embassy reception they have a bitter quarrel because Monica Faseyi is not wearing gloves. The absurdity of Dr Faseyi's attitude is revealed in remarks such as: 'Darling, if the Queen was attending a garden party, would you go dressed without gloves?' (p. 40). The quarrel subsides when the husband discovers that not many people have noticed his wife's violation of etiquette. But then she commits another 'disgrace' by refusing to drink champagne and asking for palm-wine, whereupon the husband goes round asking his friends to listen for any 'adverse comments' that people might be making about him. Nor is Doctor Faseyi the only one who worries about what everybody else is doing and saying. Kola's conversation with Monica Faseyi reveals that gossip is characteristic of this high society. When Kola introduces himself to Mrs Faseyi he discovers that she already knows that he is working on a canvas and that an angry mother has stormed into his studio because her daughter has been sitting for him.

Professor Oguazor is another pseudo-academic who is particularly careful to do everything in the English way to prove himself educated. He is luckier than Faseyi because his wife gives full co-operation and they try their best to live up to their idea of English respectability. They organize parties at which they hang up chandeliers and decorate the walls with imported plastic fruits. For Oguazor and Faseyi, academic jobs are a stepping stone to managerial and political appointments, which is why they invest so much money in social gatherings to which they invite politicians and directors of foreign firms. But the most disgraceful of the academics is Dr Lumoye, who performs illegal abortions after he has had sexual intercourse with the girls as part of his fees. When one of the university students refuses to participate in this immoral arrangement Dr Lumoye spreads damaging gossip about her around the university campus.

Soyinka's satire is not directed exclusively against the élite. The villagers are no better than the educated city-dwellers. Dehinwa's mother, who arrives at her daughter's flat in the middle of the night with a gang of relatives to admonish her about the dangers of marrying a man from another tribe, is as absurd as anyone in the novel. Soyinka is one of the few African writers who do not idealize traditional relationships or the African past. For him greed, violence, ignorance and other human follies and vices have always been a feature of society. The idealism and euphoria with which some other writers have evoked the African past he holds to be an illusion. As early as 1960 Soyinka had started warning his society against complacency. In his play, *A Dance of the Forest,* performed during the independence celebrations of Nigeria, Soyinka tried to dispel the illusions about resurrecting the ancient glories of the continent. The fears which he expressed in this play have become the reality which he portrays in a later play, *Kongi's Harvest,* as well as in this novel. The author's feelings about negritude are often expressed in passing remarks such as the one which Sagoe makes to his friends one cloudy afternoon: 'I could do with some negritude, anything to keep me warm'. When Sagoe sees a crowd chasing a thief he remembers a line in a bad poem which he had read in an 'identity' magazine: 'run, poor negro, run'. Elsewhere, talking about negritude literature, Wole Soyinka has said:

> I do not say that nothing of this literature was valid or that there was not to be found in it genuine literary value. Only that the present philosophy, the present direction of modern Africa was created by politicians, not writers, and is this not a contradiction in a society whose great declaration to the outside world is that of a super-abundant humanism?[8]

Judging by recent trends in African fiction many writers seem to share this view. Even a writer such as Camara Laye who has often been charged with sentimentality about the past, has, in his latest novel, portrayed an African society controlled by selfishness, greed and a disregard for human suffering.[9] Recent writers such as Ayi Kwei Armah, Cameron Duodu, Robert Serumaga and David Rubadiri all paint pictures of African societies in which violence, suffering, greed and ineptitude loom large. The section of society which is criticized most is that of politicians. Less and less do the artist and the politician share a common outlook on the destiny of their society. The artist is increasingly reluctant to give his voice for the recital of political slogans. This growing difference in outlook is reflected in the way the image of the politician grows worse and worse in the African novel. The politician is commonly portrayed as a self-seeking, vain, fraudulent, and ignorant demagogue. Uncle Taiwo of *Jagua Nana,*[10] Chozo, of *No Bride Price,*[11] Koomson of *The Beautyful Ones Are Not Yet Born*[12] and Sir Derinola of *The Interpreters* all belong to this group.

Chief Nanga of *A Man of the People* is another of their kind though he has some positive qualities too. He has a charming, charismatic and gregarious personality. Though he is unscrupulous in his pursuit of personal interests, he is astute and cunning, and finds it easy to influence people. He is a truly Machiavellian hero whose pursuit of personal goals is unhampered by any moral scruples but who maintains the loyalty of those he exploits.

After about ten years as an obscure Member of Parliament, Chief Nanga sees a new opportunity when the Cabinet is split by an economic crisis. Because the then Minister of Finance counsels austere economic measures which might reduce the popularity of the party, he is dismissed by the Prime Minister, along with two-thirds of the Cabinet. In the Parliamentary debate which follows this crisis Chief Nanga distinguishes himself as a heckler. According to the narrator:

> If anyone had cared to sum up Mr Nanga's interruptions they would have made a good hour's continuous yelp. (p. 5)

No one hears what the Minister of Finance has to say because Mr Nanga and other M.P.s who are trying to prove their loyalty to the Prime Minister drown the speech with interruptions such as 'they deserve to be hanged', 'they have bitten the finger with which their mother fed them'. The Prime Minister carries the day and Mr Nanga is subsequently given a cabinet appointment. Thus begins a career of long tours round the country, accompanied by extravagant ceremonies, numerous foreign visits, the accumulation of a large personal fortune and the endless seduction of young women, married and single alike.

Because Mr Nanga and his colleagues are incapable of giving direction to the affairs of the country the economic crisis worsens. The government increases import duties by twenty per cent. This provokes a countrywide outcry against the government, and the Prime Minister is forced to call for fresh elections. Election fraud by the government leads to an outbreak of violence in which some members of the Cabinet lose their lives while the rest are locked up by the army which takes over power. Chief Nanga thus falls from power six years after his appointment as a Minister. The novel depicts and satirizes Chief Nanga's success during these six years of fame and popularity.

When the novel opens we see Chief Nanga at the height of his popularity. 'No one can deny that Chief the Honourable M. A. Nanga, M.P., was the most approachable politician in the country. Whether you asked in the city or in his home village, Anata, they would tell you that he was a man of the people,' says the narrator at the beginning of the story, explaining the enthusiasm with which Nanga is greeted when he visits his home village.

He returns the praise of the crowd by flattering them, by putting on an act of humility and by offering help to some of the villagers. He picks on Odili to show his generosity and speaks loudly enough to be overheard by the crowd, which includes journalists:

> 'By the way, Odili, I think you are wasting your talent here. I want you to come to the capital and take up a strategic post in the civil service. We shouldn't leave everything to the highland tribes . . . our people must press for their own share of the national cake.' (p. 12)

Nepotism has become so established in the system that it can be cheered at public meetings. If the people are told that it is wrong for a man to use his position to enrich himself or to help his friends and supporters they will ask 'if a sensible man would spit out the juicy morsel that good fortune placed in his mouth?' For men like Nanga the nation is a cake from which each group should try to get as large a share as possible. As A. Y. Andoh has pointed out, a successful politician in a modern African state is regarded as an investment by his tribal group:

> The wide extension of kinship bonds means that a chief (or any other official) is frequently put into the position of having to choose between his obligations to favour particular kinsmen and his official duty to act disinterestedly. This type of conflict of obligation is quite real for the politician, civil servant, policeman or even judge. For a successful political candidate is regarded by many of his constituents (frequently his kinsmen) as an investment, and will be asked for jobs or scholarships, or for help in local disputes.[13]

This analysis is also supported by E. Wallerstein in his essay 'Ethnicity and National Integration in West Africa'. He states:

> The dysfunctional aspects of ethnicity for national integration are obvious. They are basically two. The first is that ethnic groups are still particularistic in their orientation and diffuse in their obligation, even if they are less so than the extended family. The ethnic roles are insufficiently segregated from the occupational and political roles because of the extensiveness of the ethnic group. Hence we have the resulting familiar problems of nepotism and corruption.[14]

But to return to the novel. There are many incidents involving corruption and the misuse of public funds. We are told for example that each minister has a residence of seven bedrooms and seven bathrooms. In addition Nanga owns three blocks of seven-storey luxury flats, which he has built at three thousand pounds each in his wife's name. This contrasts sharply with the general poverty in the country which we get a glimpse of when Odili tells us about his experiences as a houseboy in Giligili. The sanitary conditions are so bad that the villagers can 'hear' the smell of the lavatory bucket ten miles away. This is how Odili recalls his experience:

> The only excitement I remember in Giligili was our nightly war on rats. We had two rooms in the large iron-roofed house with its earth walls and floor. My sister, her husband and two small children slept in one and the rest of us—three boys—shared the other with bags of rice, garri, beans and other foodstuff. And of course the rats. (p. 41)

This description is in strong contrast to that of the bedroom in Chief Nanga's house only a few pages earlier:

> I was simply hypnotized by the luxury of the great suite assigned to me. When I lay down in the double bed that seemed to ride on a cushion of air, and switched on that reading lamp and saw all the beautiful furniture anew from a lying down position and looked beyond the door to the gleaming bathroom and the towels as large as *lappa* I had to confess that if I were at that moment made a minister I would be most anxious to remain one for ever. (p. 37)

The man who lives in the luxury described above continues to amass even more property while the poor people in the villages get poorer and poorer. What interests the novelist are the features of a society in which such exploitation can go on for so long without anyone raising a finger and in which the leaders continue exploiting when they have far more than they need. Self-seeking and inhumanity are sanctioned in a way they would have been in a traditional society, held together by a strong moral tradition. The survival of this tradition in the village is well illustrated by the Josiah-Azoge incident. Josiah, a shopkeeper, steals the stick of Azoge, a blind man. The blind man realizes that his stick has been exchanged for another and calls upon the whole village to come to his aid. The village reacts by boycotting Josiah's shop and ostracizing him socially. As one of the villagers says: 'Josiah has taken enough for the owner to notice.' The owner is the collective will of the village. The village is held together by a strong moral law which no one can violate without running the risk of facing heavy social sanctions from the community as a whole. But moral considerations do not enter the affairs of the nation. The nation as a whole has no moral traditions. This is why it is possible for the same Josiah to return to the village during the parliamentary election campaign to receive the cheers of the same villagers. The author makes an important observation that the moral power which unites the village does not unite the nation. In fact it makes it difficult for national institutions to be accorded any respect because the nation is thought of as no more than a cake to be scrambled for. This is why soon after independence the political regime quickly degenerates into a scramble for power and position, and public servants are recruited on the basis of *whom* rather than *what* they know.

But political disorder is only one aspect of social decay. The society has been invaded by a wide range of values which have destroyed the traditional balance between the material and the spiritual spheres of life, which has led inevitably to the hypocrisy of double standards. This has already been discussed in relation to the Josiah incident and it can be traced in the lives of all the characters in the novel. Odili himself, the man who judges others, is the most hypocritical. Although he has moral objections to Nanga's political conduct he finds himself shouting 'Hear! Hear!' to the latter's specious remarks at Anata Grammar School, then adds asides like: 'I like to think that I meant it to be sarcastic' (p. 10), or: 'This time I clearly meant my tongue to be in my cheek'. As soon as Odili is offered a holiday in the Minister's house he becomes reconciled to, or is willing to forget Nanga's political views. The fact is that Odili is all the time courting favours from Chief Nanga but he does not want to acknowledge it. He is always rationalizing motives and most of his actions are insincere. When he first decides to engage in political action he explains it to himself in these words:

> I must say that I was immediately taken with the idea of the Common People's Convention. Apart from everything else it would add a second string to my bow when I came to deal with Nanga. But right now I was anxious not to appear to Max and his friends as the easily impressed type. I suppose I wanted to erase whatever impression was left of Max's unfortunate if unintentional presentation of me as a kind of pitiable jellyfish. So I made what I intended to be a little spirited sceptical speech. (p. 78)

Odili is caught between his principles, his desire to see things running well in the country on the one hand, and his vanity and selfishness on the other. This situation is no doubt partly due to the kind of education he has had, which has distanced him from the reality of his society. Max tries to make him see this reality. But Max too finds himself in a dilemma which leads him into hypocrisy. He is trying to rid the country of corruption and the yoke of foreign capitalism but finds that he has to accept money from a communist country. He has to convince himself that this is safer but, of course, we know it to be an illusion. When the campaign starts he finds that he has to accept money from Chief Koko, his opponent, and then later rationalizes the act by telling Odili: 'Now you tell me how you propose to fight such a dirty war without soiling your hands a little.' The last word is ironical for it is this 'little' incident which embitters Chief Koko who is later to plot the murder of Max.

In a society where the traditional moral order has been disrupted it is impossible to escape from double standards, of which the whole society is guilty. As has been pointed out earlier, in the village of Anata, Josiah is ostracized for having cheated a blind man, but when the same Josiah returns to the village in the entourage of Chief Nanga's campaigners he is cheered. The irrationality of applying different moral values to the two situations is not apparent to the villagers who have not yet learnt to take the idea of the nation seriously. In the same way the nation as a whole does not realize its own hypocrisy in being prepared to denounce anybody as soon as they have fallen from power. Only when Nanga's regime has been overthrown is there a general outcry against the excesses of that regime, and we might be reminded that Nanga himself had gained power as a result of the general outcry against the Finance Minister and all his enlightened colleagues who were dismissed by the Prime Minister at the beginning of the novel.

Odili, Max, Nanga and the whole society are trapped in a situation of conflicting moral values where the areas of duty, self-sacrifice, and service to the community are all still undefined. The nation is a pressure-cooker of social experiment and it is uncertain whether the pot will contain the pressure or burst.

The social situation of *The Interpreters* is simply sterile. In *A Man of the People* at least we know that there are potential elements of regeneration. We know there are patriotic politicians who have been silenced and we see some young idealists trying to change the situation. In *The Interpreters* on the other hand the intellectuals are the most decadent group in society. The national university is the place where aristocratic social gatherings are arranged while the rest of the nation is starving. Nor are these parties simply a reflection of the relative affluence of the university community. They reflect completely foreign values and are organized in a style that is foreign to Nigeria. The values of this community reflected at social gatherings show the university to be a foreign body far removed from the interests of the society in which it is situated.

It is this general decadence that inspires Sagoe's philosophy of voidancy. This philosophy has it that 'to shit is human, but to voidate is divine'. To voidate becomes a means of release and self-communion as well as a means of revenging oneself upon the rotten system. It also becomes a symbolic purification of the self. The externalization of this rottenness can be seen in detailed descriptions of polluted atmospheres such as Sagoe encounters on his way to Sir Derinola's funeral.

> Sagoe encountered first the deserted nightcart and trailer; some distance behind, its contents were spread on the road. To reconstruct the accident the enormous porthole had flown open and the driver had not stopped fast enough. Over twenty yards were spread huge pottage mounds,

> twenty yards of solid and running, plebeian and politician, indigenous and foreign shit. Right on the tarred road. (p. 108)

Sagoe is so obsessed with shit that he takes a photograph of this scene and offers it to his editor for publication. The editor of course refuses. Nwabuzor is a man who has decided to do anything for money. He has given up cherishing ideals about human relationships. That is why he advises Sagoe to do whatever work he is given because in the end every man is working for himself. Oddly enough it is people like Nwabuzor, with the knowledge to run the system, who have given up trying to influence the direction of affairs in their society and it is the ignorant people like Chief Winsala who assert themselves. So the whole country is smeared with the filth of their blunders, outwardly represented by the display and smell of the lavatory bucket, the contents of which are often subjected to the close scrutiny of Sagoe. The image recurs in West African fiction—for instance there is the village of Giligili in *A Man of the People*, where villagers complain of 'hearing' the smell of the lavatory bucket ten miles from the village.

It is not only the public life of the country that has been affected by the moral crisis. Even people's private relationships have been corrupted. For example, Dehinwa's affair with Sagoe suffers from being a mixture of sterile traditionalism and empty modernism—they are modern enough to sleep together in Dehinwa's flat but too traditional to make love before they are married.

At the beginning of the second part of the novel our attention is switched from the social problems of Nigeria to Kola's progress in creating a Pantheon which is to become an expression of his view of man's place in the world. The interest of all the interpreters focuses on Kola's work because it promises to organize the experience which they have gone through so far and thus give them a better understanding of themselves. The reader follows the progress of the painting with similar interest because the completion of the canvas will provide a creative interpretation of the interpreters' experience by someone who has been part of that experience and who is the most perceptive of the whole group.

The delay in the completion of the Pantheon is caused by Kola's search for what he feels to be a missing element. Since the canvas portrays both gods and men he needs a bridge between heaven and earth to link up the two sets of beings. It is this quest for the missing element that interests Kola in Lazarus.

Several critics have expressed the view that the Lazarus story does not fit into the artistic design of the novel. These critics have failed to see that Lazarus is one of the interpreters. His bizarre prophetism is his own means of escaping from both the moral emptiness of his society and his social limitations. Seen objectively, his behaviour is no more eccentric than Sagoe's voidancy, Egbo's mysticism or Sekoni's 'dome of continuity'. All these characters have been driven by frustrated spiritual yearnings into eccentric modes of self-expression. Lazarus makes the most daring attempt to transcend his human limitations by trying to link himself with the supernatural. He tries to transform men so that the better part of their nature can prevail over the baser part. He seeks out criminals and tries to turn them into saints.

Lazarus shares with the rest of the interpreters the desire to transform and to play a creative role in the world. He makes a much more vigorous attempt to be a god. Kola chooses him to be the link between gods and men in the chain of creation on his canvas and this completes the canvas. In Lazarus Kola sees most clearly the eternal frustration of man, his desire to be something greater than himself and the inevitable comedy which results from his attempts because it is impossible for man to realise this aspiration. This links up with the social dilemma in which the interpreters find themselves in the novel. Kola sees this dilemma to be part of the eternal process of man's attempt to overcome or come to terms with his limitations. The problem may take on different aspects at different times and in different places but its basic nature remains the same, namely man's quest for the omnipotence which has been denied him in creation: and this is the central theme of Kola's Pantheon. In the description of the Pantheon we hear of 'the first apostate rolling the boulder down the back of the unsuspecting deity—for they must learn the first stab in the back and keep inferiors harmless within sight. . . .' (p. 224). In other words, in order to be on the safe side, gods have deliberately set limits to man's ability to control his world. Man's capabilities have been fixed by some higher power that is jealous of him.

The vision of Man's destiny which is expressed in Kola's Pantheon is a mixture of Yoruba, Greek and Christian mythologies. The Yoruba story of creation is blended with the Christian story of the destruction of the world by flood. The Christian story of resurrection is superimposed. The picture is deliberately confused to stress the impossibility of man's understanding his origin and destiny with any sense of finality. The mixing of mythologies of such highly divergent origins is a comment on the essential oneness of man's fate through the ages and in different places. Egbo complains about the canvas that the artist 'has made the beginning itself a resurrection. This is the optimist's delusion of continuity.' But the canvas is not optimistic. On the contrary the elements of pessimism preponderate in that there is an insistence on man's inability to change his situation in the world; time and place seem only to alter the form of his perennial problems. All human actions are absurd gestures which ultimately change nothing. Art is the ultimate consolation because it enables man to understand himself and through this understanding to reconcile himself to his situation and through his imagination to transcend his limitations.

Lazarus is the central figure on the canvas, the bridge between heaven and earth. He is referred to as 'the vomit-streak of the heavenly serpent', representing man as a base form of the divine essence. He is made the link in the chain of creation; but he is also drawn in arched form in the colours of the rainbow to represent God's covenant with Noah: that the world would never be destroyed by water again. The rainbow form of the bridge thus suggests the threat of destruction through fire. One is reminded of James Baldwin's essay, *The Fire Next Time*,[15] which uses the same Christian mythology to interpret history. The essay ends by quoting the song of a slave: 'God gave Noah the rainbow sign, No more water, the fire next time!' One can't help thinking that the names Noah and Lazarus were deliberately chosen by Soyinka because of their Biblical associations. Noah is rejected by Kola because, like the mythological Noah, he is a completely neutral figure. Lazarus, a name which we associate with material deprivation, spiritual anguish and physical suffering, is adopted, and he is rising from his grave, reaching out to the sky. This complex image seems to suggest that when change comes next it will take the form of a revolution in which the down-trodden members of the society will rise against their incompetent masters.

The completion of Kola's Pantheon forms the climax of the novel. It brings together all the experiences which the characters have shared. After celebrating its completion they have nothing more to hold them together and they each go their way. Thus, Kola is the chief 'interpreter', the one who works out some meaning in the lives of all the characters. One cannot help identifying the vision of the painter with that of the author of the novel. The reflections which pass through Kola's mind about the nature of art on thc night of the exhibition seem appropriate for the completion of both the painting and the novel. Kola says:

> But at least I can record my intimations of these presences have been too momentary and they come in disjointed fragments, that is why I have taken so long. . . . (p. 228)

Although *The Interpreters* could not be described as 'disjointed fragments' it suffers from a lack of strict artistic discipline. Many of the episodes and incidents which make up the novel have considerable dramatic power and are poetically conceived but they are not always tailored to fit into the artistic design of the novel. Much of the Lazarus story could have been cut out without great loss to the novel. So could many passages on voidancy. But if the novel suffers from a lack of strict economy it gains much from abundance and variety of characters, scenes and incidents. The use of different art forms—painting by Kola, carving by Sekoni and singing by Joe Golder—all these things extend dimensions of the novel.

At the end neither the young group of intellectuals nor Lazarus have changed their society. All they have done is gain an understanding of their lives. All this understanding is brought together in the Pantheon. It is therefore not surprising that the night when the completion of the Pantheon is celebrated is also 'the night of severance' when the interpreters must part. At the exhibition Bandele sits 'like a timeless image brooding over lesser beings'. The disillusionment and understanding of the interpreters as they move about in the exhibition room contrasts with the sterile gossip of the university lecturers who use the occasion to exchange slanderous remarks about their students. However, the understanding which the interpreters gain through art can only be a consolation. At the beginning of the novel they are talking in terms of changing the social reality of their country. At the end they have given this up and only talk in terms of expressing their frustration through art, just as Sekoni, who tried hard to put his ideas into practice, was defeated by the system and finally turned to sculpture. Art becomes a means of expressing the ugliness of the reality which the individual cannot change. But through this the artist is able to make a permanent statement which he could not have made through active participation in politics.

Both *A Man of the People* and *The Interpreters* are indictments of African society after independence. They portray this society as one riddled with greed, violence and ignorance from which there is no apparent way of escape. These novels paint a darker picture of African society than the novels which depict the same society during the period of transition from colonial rule to independence. Even *No Longer At Ease* which had none of the optimism we find in *The African* or the glorious martyrdom of *A Wreath for Udomo* ends with the protagonist being sentenced to a few months imprisonment. The events in *A Man of the People* on the other hand lead to widespread violence and bloodshed that leave the society in much greater uncertainty. Since the publication of the two novels discussed in this chapter African writing has been growing progressively more pessimistic; angry artists, if they cannot point out solutions to the problems which face the continent today, have at least attacked the errors and villainy of the politicians and the people. It would appear that Achebe was expressing the view of many African novelists when he said:

> We must seek the freedom to express our thoughts and our feelings, even against ourselves, without the anxiety that what we say might be taken as evidence against our race. We have stood in the dock for too long pleading and protesting before ruffians and frauds masquerading as disinterested judges.[16]

NOTES

1. Achebe, Chinua, 'The Black Writer's Burden', *Présence Africaine*, vol. 31, no. 59, Paris, 1966, p. 138.
2. Achebe, Chinua, *A Man of the People*, African Writers Series, Heinemann Educational Books Ltd, London, 1966.
3. For the support of this view, see Andoh, A., 'Background to Government and Politics in Africa', *Présence Africaine*, 2nd Quarter, no. 74, 1970, pp. 29–45.
4. Wallerstein, Emmanuel, *The Road to Independence*, La Haye, Mouton, 1964, p. 147.
5. Lloyd, C. P., *Africa in Social Change*, Penguin, London, 1967.
6. Serumaga, Robert, *Return to the Shadows*, African Writers Series, Heinemann Educational Books Ltd, London, 1970 (1969).
7. Ghali, Waguih, *Beer in the Snooker Club*, André Deutsch, London, 1964.
8. Soyinka, Wole, 'The Writer in an Afrian State', *Transition*, vol. 6, no. 31, Kampala, July 1967, p. 12.
9. Laye, Camara, *A Dream of Africa*, Collins, London, 1968.
10. Ekwensi, Cyprian, *Jagua Nana*, African Writers Series, Heinemann Educational Books Ltd, London, 1975 (1961).
11. Rubadiri, David, *No Bride Price*, East African Publishing House, Nairobi, 1967.
12. Armah, Ayi Kwei, *The Beautyful Ones Are Not Yet Born*, African Writers Series, Heinemann Educational Books Ltd, London, 1969 (1968).
13. Andoh, A. Y., 'Background to Government and Politics in Africa', *Présence Africaine*, no. 74, 1970, p. 4.
14. Lloyd, P. C., *op. cit.*
15. Baldwin, James, *The Fire Next Time*, New York, 1963.
16. Achebe, 'The Black Writer's Burden', *op. cit.*, p. 139.

5. Freedom as Nightmare

Armah's *The Beautyful Ones Are Not Yet Born*

By far the bleakest picture yet painted by a novel about the sourness of African independence is that in Ayi Kwei Armah's *The Beautyful Ones Are Not Yet Born**. So overwhelming is the sense of decay which is created in the novel that the death-cycle of life becomes the reflecting medium in which everything is observed. The vision of the author comes dangerously close to the edge of despair. We are presented with a world in which the sewage pipes of history have exploded and everything is polluted. The senses of the reader are vigorously assaulted to the point of being numbed by the persistent imagery of decay, putrefaction and death. We meet a child, its nose overflowing with mucus and its mother sucking it with her mouth; we meet a young woman, her body disfigured by 'creases of a prematurely tired skin'. We are not sure whether she is a horse or human, dead or alive. Streets are littered with rubbish that overflows from dustbins onto the pavements, bannisters on building stairs are coated with vast accumulations of dirt, and lavatory walls are streaked with organic brown matter 'about the level of the adult anus'. Everybody is described as sweating, coughing, spitting. 'All around decaying things push inward and mix all the body's juices with the taste of rot.' (p. 40). The stench of putrefying matter becomes one with the stench of despair in the men who are walking about. The sounds, the smells, the sights and the thoughts of the people all mingle into a single rhythm of decay and death.

Irving Howe said of Orwell's *Nineteen Eighty Four*:

> About some books we feel that our reluctance to return to them is the true measure of our admiration. It is hard to suppose that many people go back, from a spontaneous desire, to read *Nineteen Eighty Four*: there is neither reason nor need to, no one forgets it. The usual distinctions between forgotten details and a vivid general impression mean nothing

*Armah, Ayi Kwei, *The Beautyful Ones Are Not Yet Born*, African Writers Series, Heinemann Educational Books Ltd, London, 1969 (1968). (Page references are to the reset 1975 edition.)

> here, for the book is written out of one passionate breath, each word is bent to a severe discipline of meaning, everything is stripped to the bareness of terror.[1]

One only need substitute 'horror' for 'terror' and the remarks become appropriate to *The Beautyful Ones Are Not Yet Born.* There is an acute similarity in the way both novels are organized with 'a severe discipline' to evoke a reality which to many readers must appear distinctly one-sided. They share a terrible frankness which often becomes a severe strain upon the senses. Orwell employs the symbol of dust to conjure up a sense of desolation and the erosion of the human spirit. Armah uses excrement and putrefaction to conjure up a spectre of life as a death-cycle.

The effect of the novel is achieved through a gradual build-up of detailed symbolic descriptions of isolated objects and situations so that each description in some way reflects an aspect of the decaying process with which the world of the novel is cluttered. At the beginning we follow the headlights of a bus as they sweep round in a curve until they come to a stop on a specific object. The same cinematic technique is used throughout the novel. The author gives us a rapid impression of places and events and then concentrates our attention on specific details. In the opening episode of the novel we are rushed through an account of incidents at a bus-stop before attention is focused on the inside of the bus where the conductor and one passenger are sitting, together but unaware of each other. The conductor is gloating over the contents of his collecting bag. The careful attention which he pays to the different forms of currency betrays a strange perversion. He regards the physical form of money as an object of pleasure. He not only examines the different colours of the various currency forms, he feels their texture and sniffs them affectionately, then he checks the earnings of the evening against the tickets so that he can appropriate the surplus. The passenger, who is throughout the novel referred to as 'the man', is fast asleep though his eyes are wide-open. This sleep and loneliness are symbolic of the man's isolation and withdrawal from his social world. His financial deprivation is made apparent by his lack of a handkerchief. Every physical detail and gesture has a symbolic value. As the man moves through the town towards his office through the littered streets our attention is focused on the overflowing dustbins surrounded by piles of rubbish.

By this skilful selection of incidents and objects, within relatively few pages, the author has established a social and physical world which is completely encased in dirt, and threatened by death. The bus in which the man is travelling moves with 'an endless spastic shudder, as if its pieces were held together by too much rust ever to fall completely apart', the people are coughing and spitting out blobs of mucus and even bank notes have a rotten smell. Bodily excretion, rust, decay—both physical and moral—work in mutual conspiracy to imprison the man and the world in which he lives. Anything that is clean appears like an anomaly in this environment. Thus the multi-storied hotel, the Atlantic Caprice, stands out on the top of the hill as 'an insulting white'. The name of the hotel has clear association with exploitation.

The people who move in this death cave are described as sleep-walkers. 'The walkers sleep still, but their nightmares in which they are dwarfs unable to run away and little insects caught in endless pools, these fearful dreams are gone.' (p. 2). Thus only the man is continually aware of his nightmare. The rest of the people have learnt to adapt themselves to their condition and to regard their polluted environment as a natural one.

The early part of the story has a haunting power which derives from its allegorical character. The people have no names and places remain unspecified. The man becomes the Everyman of folk literature. The story also borrows additional power from the modernistic technique of fusing mental and physical descriptions so that they dissolve into one cathartic movement. However, later in the novel things begin to become more particular and characters are more individualized. We are made aware that the events relate to Ghana. This creates unease in the mind of the reader because it demands a different level of response from him. We are unwilling to accept the story at the level of social realism because that would call for a more balanced portrayal of life than the author affords us in the novel. This creates conflicting demands upon the reader's sensibilities and thus diffuses the power of the story. It is difficult to find the basis for R. W. Noble's response to the novel when he writes:

> *The Beautyful Ones Are Not Yet Born* unites, with striking effectiveness, qualities of technique and form from three different traditions of fiction. The tone of style of the pithily imagined dialogue between the universally designated characters, 'the man' and 'the teacher', are evolved from the African oral tradition of story-telling, and similar qualities are present in some recent writing such as Hamidou Kane's *Ambiguous Adventure*. The literary tradition of realism is reflected in the plausible pattern of social, political, and physical detail. Deriving from the modernist movement is the minute exploration of the timeless motion of the individual mind: its fears, temptations, uncertainties, sufferings, guilt and loneliness. Ayi Kwei Armah thus achieves a complex style which aptly conveys the inner moral and outer social conflicts of West African reality.[2]

Even if we accept the superficial designations and glib comments on the various elements of style, Mr Noble's conclusion appears too voluble. There is no harmonious synthesis of the various narrative styles. The generalized qualities of folk-lore and the modernist symbolic descriptions work together quite effectively as long as we do not expect social plausibility. The attempt to fix the story and to weave it into recent Ghanaian history appears to be an intrusive urge on the author's part to release his rage and disgust at his country's politics. There are many passages which one could not take at their face value as 'the inner moral and outer social conflicts of West African reality'. Here, for example, is a description of the physical atmosphere inside the office where the man works:

> The wetness within came partly from the sea which was only a little way away. Sometimes it was possible to taste very clearly the salt that had been eating the walls and the paint on them, if one cared to run one's hand down the dripping surfaces and taste the sticky mess. Partly, too, the wetness came from people, everybody who worked in the office. Everybody seemed to sweat a lot, not from the exertion of their jobs, but from some kind of inner struggle that was always going on. So the sea salt and sweat together and the fan above made this stewy atmosphere in which the suffering sleepers came and worked and went dumbly back afterwards to homes they had earlier fled. There was really no doubt that it was like that in all their homes. . . . (p. 20)

Even the most one-sided indictment of Nkrumah's regime can hardly justify the claim that under that regime most people were suffering sleepers who had to flee from their homes because they were too deprived to fulfil family obligations, and that they sweated permanently 'from the exertion of an inner struggle that was always going on'. What makes it even more difficult for the reader to accept these intrusive comments is the lack of identity of the speaking voice. In the first five chapters the story is told by a third person narrator who generally follows the main character and interprets the world from his point of view. Then suddenly, in the sixth chapter, a first person narrator takes over. And yet, throughout the novel, we never discover what relationship this 'I' narrator has with the third person narrator. Later the two narrators merge but a certain ambiguity remains as to whether we are seeing the world from the point of vicw of the man or from the point of view of the indeterminate narrator.

The very complexity of the narrative style and the multiple characters of the speaking voice seem to weaken the story by confusing levels of response in the reader's mind. One can't help agreeing with Eldred Jones when he says of the novel:

> The earlier vagueness and anonymity combine to give the earlier part a peculiar effectiveness. If this was a deliberate effect sought by the author it is difficult to see why he chose to become increasingly particular. The character of the novel changes as a result, without seeming to gain much from the change.[3]

It would appear that the occasional switch from allegory to social realism comes from the author's impulse to use the novel as a platform for denouncing Nkrumah's regime. Apart from the fact that Nkrumah's fall is a very risky subject for fiction because of its political currency, if it were to be used at all then the artist would have to afford us a special insight into the political and social issues which led to the downfall. Merely to say that the regime was corrupt is to oversimplify by adopting second-rate opinions. Between 1963 and 1973 there were well over 30 military *coups d'état* in Africa. The events of the continent seem to be following a pattern, so that the explanation of any one coup in terms of the personality of one leader appears inadequate, even in so far as specifically political issues are concerned. Besides, it appears arrogant for the artist to set himself apart and to denounce sections of the community as if he himself were above all of them. Very often the outbursts against Ghanaian leaders are charged with personal bitterness and self-righteous indignation. The novel dismisses the black élite as slaves of the colonial boss and their only ambition to take over the privileges of their former masters. The tendency to generalize figures may also be seen at its weakest here:

> These men who were to lead us out of our despair, they came like men already grown fat and cynical with the eating of centuries of power they had never struggled for, old before they had even been born into power, and ready only for the grave. They were lawyers before, something grown greasy on the troubles of people who worked the land, but now they were out to be our saviours. Their brothers and their friends were merchants eating what was left in the teeth of the white men with their companies. They too came to speak to us of salvation. Our masters were the white men and we were coming to know this, and the knowledge was filling us with fear first and then with anger. And they who would be our leaders, they also had their white men for their masters, and they also feared the masters, but after the fear what was at the bottom of their beings was not the hate and the anger we knew in our despair. What they felt was love. What they felt for their white masters and our white masters was gratitude and faith. And they had come to us at last, to lead us and to guide us to promised tomorrows. (p. 81)

It is not surprising therefore that an African reviewer reacted to this kind of writing in these terms:

> So why this artistic arrogance? It seems to me that the author had worried himself sick before he wrote the novel: all right, I'm African, but what have I to show for it? All right, Ghana is my country, but what has she given me, to make her presence a reality? All right, THEY are my leaders, but what sort of people are they? All right, I should be a man of THE PEOPLE (that mythical entity!) but what have they done to me? All right, I should speak to my people in their own language, but when did they encourage me to do so?[4]

When in the middle of the narration we suddenly read: 'How long will Africa be accursed with its leaders?' we cannot help thinking that the narrator is merely being used as a mouthpiece for recrimination. Nkrumah himself has blamed African political instability upon the collaboration between 'The African foreign-dominated middle class' and external agents.[5] The military élite and the intellectual élite are seen as part of this middle class. Nkrumah himself evidently sees himself as much outside this class as does Kwei Armah, and attacks basically the same group of people.

The murky ambience of the novel, both physical and moral, is only valid when it is distanced as allegory or when it is presented as an aspect of the man's mind. It is indeed at this level that we accept the novel. Fortunately, the interruptions of the seemingly objective first-person narrator remain limited so that we can disregard them as intrusions of propaganda. The more universal concerns of the novel are the effects of human lust for power and money when these are given free rein in a society. Then the sense of community and mutual respect is shattered and every man relies on the self-seeking unscrupulous aspects of his nature to secure his position in that society.

> How was it possible for a man to control himself, when the admiration of the world, the pride of his family and his own secret happiness, at least for the moment, all demanded that he lose control of himself and behave like someone he was not and would never be? Money. Power. (p. 115)

In the world of the novel, wealth and power have become the principal pursuits, and the inevitable result of the situation is a complete disregard of any moral or social considerations in the drive to satisfy individual desires. But it is not man's nature which is at fault—this is how the novel escapes being negative—it is the nature of the society which calls into service the baser part of man's nature, which in a normal situation is restrained by social sanctions, human affections and responsibilities to one's community. But when the balance is disturbed society unleashes man's savagery upon himself. In this context the rise and fall of Nkrumah is seen as part of a complex process of social decay and the personal decline of the statesman is fitted into the rhythm of a wider process of disintegration. The decline of society is traced far back into the colonial period. We are told of the general suffering and social misery which characterized this period of history. Worst of all is the fact that the exploited people were forced to fight in the white man's war. This war affects the lives of the characters in a tragic manner. Kofi Billy loses his leg in the war, finds that he cannot be accommodated in the misery of post-war society and is eventually driven to take his own life. In the crime wave which is the concomitant of the post-war economic depression, Agya Akon, because he is quiet and generous, is suspected of having a lot of money and is murdered by robbers.

It is against this background that the new leader rises to power. He too finds himself unwittingly collaborating with the process of general disintegration. When he comes to power he has the best intentions for his society. But power corrupts him.

> Had he followed the path traced out by his youth and kept to it, what would have prevented a younger man, one more like himself in the purity of his youth, from coming before him as more fit to keep to the path? A youth who could have lived the way he himself had lived at first, the way he never could have lived again when he became the old man and shiny things began to pull the tired body toward rest and toward decay. But that would have meant another kind of death for him, this death of which he had begun to walk in daily fear. And so his own end had also to be the end of all he had begun, and if another promise comes it cannot be the continuation of the promise he held out but which he himself consumed, utterly destroyed. Perhaps it is too cruel of us to ask that those approaching the end of the cycle should accept without fear the going and the coming of life and death. (p. 88)

The mawkish language testifies to the shoddiness of Armah's political sentiments. But the passage makes it clear that although the leader is not completely exonerated, he is only partly responsible for the situation in which he finds himself trapped. He accedes to power in a society which has been built on exploitation and in which men set money and power as the highest goals. His rise to power is thus doomed from the beginning to follow the cyclic pattern which leads towards decay. Nevertheless, he cannot escape blame for not having tried to change things. When he is canvassing for support before he comes to power he is astute enough to humble himself; but then he too grows 'fat' with power and distances himself from the people who elected him.

Occasionally the narrator indulges in simplistic moralizing, but as long as he does so without overtly trying to woo our support for a political opinion we are willing to accept his way of seeing—that is, watching from a distance—and the oversimplification of his vision can be accepted as a particular personal view.

> He was good when he had to speak to us, and liked to be with us. . . . Now all we do is sit and wait, like before he came. It must be power. I say this because he is not the only one whom power has lost. It has happened to those around him, those who were not always there for the simple sake of the power they could find. (p. 88)

It is passages like this one which redeem the story by widening the horizons of social exploration which the novel is attempting. The problems of

Ghana or any other African country cannot be simply explained in terms of the selfishness of the leaders who took over from the colonial administration. Explanations must lie deeper in the complex process of history, and in man's perennial effort to keep in balance the interests of individual men who make up a society, and the collective interests of that society. The problem is an eternal one though it may wear different faces in different places and at different times. The novel's principal weakness is that it is only really effective when it confines itself to the plane of allegory, and that it is unable to assimilate its social and political assertions at this level. Okara's *The Voice*[6] is a novel which limits itself to this plane and avoids direct social comment with the result that it has a more powerful effect upon the mind of the reader than *The Beautyful Ones Are Not Yet Born.* And yet the social message of *The Voice* is not any less clear to us. It is a forceful political fable, illuminating the inevitable sterility of a totalitarian nationalist state in which free thought is suppressed.

The Beautyful Ones Are Not Yet Born employs archetypal imagery to convey the universality of its theme. The sea symbolizes freedom, but, simultaneously its bareness and monotony is also sometimes used to stand for deprivation. On the other hand, the land, which is the region of man's life and activity, has been polluted. The narrator recounts that often in his youth he had spent many hours on the beach with his sister and friends smoking *wee.* Often they had to spend nights there, trapped between the two elements, shunning death and yet wishing to escape from life which has been fouled by man.

> It was a desperate time, still, and it was not only Kofi Billy who thought of hiding forever from the alien world impossible to hold. (p. 78)

The man is often attracted to the silence and the withdrawal of the shoreline where his loneliness can merge with and get absorbed in the larger loneliness of space. His search for calm recalls Singh's search for escape from the restlessness of his world in Naipaul's *The Mimic Men.*[7] Like the man's, Singh's search for peace is futile. The beach is used as an image of shipwreck where Singh is trapped between the loneliness of the sea and restlessness of his native island. The man's feelings while he is walking along the edge of the harbour suggest the same sense of being lost:

> The sounds of violent work grow fainter as the wind rises past him, and keeping to the edge where he can see quite far down into the sea, he walks without any hurry, not having to think about time or going back, feeling almost happy in his suspended loneliness, until he comes to a flight of stairs built into the side of the breakwater, leading down into the sea. He leans over and looks at the steps. They descend in a simple line

> all the way down, dipping into the sea until they are no longer visible from above. The man sits down, and, feeling now a slight pain at the back of his neck, throws back his head. Small clouds, very white, hold themselves, very far away, against a sky that is a pale, weak blue, and when the man looks down again into the sea the water of it looks green and deep. A sea gull, flying low, makes a single hoarse noise that disappears into the afternoon, and the white bird itself flies off into the direction of the harbour and its inaudible noise, beautiful and light on its wings. (p. 113)

The man's mood, thoughts and movements have completely merged with the elemental rhythm of the afternoon. When he holds his head back small clouds correspondingly hold themselves against the far away sky. The steps on which he is sitting descend down into the sea until they are no longer visible. This rhythm of descent is suffused in everything. The sea below is a symbol of beckoning death. This is only one example of a persistent identification of shapes, colours and sounds of natural objects as well as atmospheric moods with the moods and thoughts of characters in the novel. The deep dive which the man takes at the end of the novel is a symbolic act of self-cleansing. It also signifies surrender and acceptance of himself. After the swim the man lies on the sand to dry and after a long sleep beholds the apocryphal image of Maanan. When we last met Maanan she was shaking with enthusiasm about the promise of the new leader. Now she is broken with despair. She is searching for something which has been lost in the sand and crying 'with all the urgency in her diseased soul': 'They have mixed it all together! Everything! They have mixed everything. And how can I find it when they have mixed it all with so many other things?' (p. 180). The search in the sand marks the impossibility of the task and the repetition of 'it' recalls Okolo's search for the unidentified 'IT' in Gabriel Okara's *The Voice* in a world where it is impossible to find it. But whereas Okolo's search is a positive process which shakes the foundations of society, Maanan's search is hopeless. There is no hope for her. She will die of despair, like many other characters in the novel.

The man's act of cleansing is necessitated by his contamination through contact with Koomson. This latter is the incarnation of all forms of social pollution from which the society needs to be saved. This is why his escape has to be made through the latrine hole. In social terms he is fit only for the sewage channel. The man brings himself very close to trouble by helping Koomson. This is the price the man has to pay for having let his family get involved with Koomson's boat business. Although the man refuses to have his name used in the business he refrains from any active opposition against his wife's involvement. He is too doubtful about his own moral position to oppose her or Koomson.

I find it difficult to accept John Povey's view when he says of the man that:

> His strengths are a tough, rational certainty and a defiant morality that remains impregnable, even to the nagging of his covetous wife.[8]

Indeed the whole story is built around the conflict within the man, his struggle to resist temptation. His instinct for survival often threatens to conquer his moral integrity. Every moment in the novel leads him further and further into loneliness and self-doubt until the military coup affords him relief. However, if he had been simply defiant, as Mr Povey suggests, he would have been a much happier person. But his happiness is undermined by uncertainty and self-doubt. He often has to go to the teacher to seek comfort and assurance. At their last meeting he finds that the teacher has sunk into despair and can provide no comfort for others. While he is listening to music in the teacher's room self-doubt fills his mind:

> For the man sitting on the desk opposite, all the cool sadness seemed able to do was raise thoughts of the lonely figure finding it more and more difficult to justify his own honesty. How could he, when all around him the whole world never tired of saying there were only two types of men who took refuge in honesty—the cowards and the fools? Very often these days he was burdened with the hopeless, impotent feeling that he was not just one of these, but a hopeless combination of the two. (p. 51)

The conflict of his mind is fanned by thoughts about his family. The conflict with his wife threatens to lead to a separation from his family as is the case with the teacher. But the man loves his family too much to sacrifice it for honesty. He is saved by the coup when his endurance seems to be cracking.

It would not be accurate to describe the man as a hero without defining the term. In the world of this novel traditional heroism is not possible. The man does not believe that the human condition in which he is trapped can be changed. He therefore makes no effort to change the system—which is the only thing that could constitute what we might call 'social heroism'. His 'heroism' is more ambivalent. He struggles against himself, against temptations, both from his wife and his own self, to take a short cut to success as everybody else seems to do. He has to contend with his secret envy for those who have succeeded by taking the path of corruption which he has resisted. We hear him telling the teacher:

> 'They are using this boat thing, Teacher', he said. 'They are using it to hit me on the head every terrible day, to make me feel so useless. And the bad thing is I know they have succeeded. I am asking myself what is wrong with me. Do I have some part missing? Teacher, this Koomson

> was my own classmate. My classmate, Teacher, my classmate. So tell me, what is wrong with me?' (p. 57)

One is inclined to think that in fact the novelist has overstated the moral weakness of the man without a counterbalancing emphasis on the qualities of mind which enable him to hold out to the end.

However, by his stoic endurance the man does achieve a kind of heroism. By the end he has been reconciled to his family, more important to him than public attainments and financial success. His manhood had been seriously challenged in his home by his failure to justify his own way of life. Now justification is provided for him by the *coup*. But in the social and political life of the country nothing changes. As soon as the man has undergone his symbolic cleansing he returns to the road only to witness another incident of corruption. The narrator intrudes to add a rather superfluous comment:

> It would be wrong, very wrong, to think as he was already thinking, that the change would bring nothing new. In the life of the nation itself, maybe nothing really new would happen. New men would take into their hands the power to steal the nation's riches and to use it for their own satisfaction. That, of course, was to be expected. New people would use the country's power to get rid of men and women who talked a language that did not flatter them. There would be nothing different in that. That would only be a continuation of the Ghanaian way of life. But here was the real change. The individual man of power now shivering, his head filled with the fear of the vengeance of those he had wronged. For him everything was going to change. And for those like him who had grown greasy and fat singing the praises of their chief, for those who had been getting themselves ready for the enjoyment of hoped-for favors, there would be long days of pain ahead. The flatterers with their new white Mercedes cars would have to find ways of burying old words. For those who had come directly against the old power, there would be much happiness. But for the nation itself there would be only a change of embezzlers and a change of the hunters and the hunted. (p. 162)

This then is the dark reality which the novel paints as man's condition. The explicit comment says even more than the action of the novel gives us reason to concern ourselves with. The novelist fears that he has not sufficiently hammered home his disgust with humanity, especially the African part of it and in particular, Ghana. So wicked, so dirty and so corrupt is humanity that there is no point in the individual's trying to change it. The individual has got to learn to live in the midst of the filth and must try to secure his own private salvation, through endurance. In this unalterable situation the artist's position is like the position of the teacher in the novel. He is compared to one of the inmates of Plato's cave who at last manages to turn and get a glimpse of the light outside the cave.

When he turns back and tries to tell the other inmates about what he has seen outside, they respond by saying that his long absence has made him mad.

The end of the novel confirms the title, that the beautiful ones are not yet born. Those who are already born are corrupt, greedy, selfish and dishonest. But within the statement of the title itself is implied some kind of hope—that the beautiful ones might be born. But this is uncertain. Hence the ambiguity of the very beautiful flower in the middle of the oval inscription:

THE BEAUTYFUL ONES
ARE NOT YET BORN

The flower is 'solitary, unexplainable, and very beautiful'. In terms of the vision which the novel presents, the meaning of this flower remains obscure. But earlier in the novel the third person narrator whom we identify with the author has already said:

> Yet out of the decay and the dung there is always a new flowering. Perhaps it helps to know that. (p. 85)

The reader is simply asked to imagine that there might be a flowering in the future, that all the filth and decaying process which is described might form manure for a new healthy growth.

The man contemplates the meaning of this disturbing image until it is imperceptibly replaced by the melodious note of a bird singing on the top of a latrine pit. That is how life should be taken, so the experience seems to suggest. The sound, like the lonely flower, is isolated, surrounded by a hostile element. Man too is a stranger in this hostile and ugly world. But the alienation which the man experiences is not that of the hero of Camus' *L'Etranger*.* In Camus' novel the hero cannot find a sense of purpose in the universe, while in Armah's novel the protagonist sees a moral pattern which is clear but impossible to live by because the political and social set-up denies it.

The man is a symbol of the alienation of the individual in an authoritarian state. There is no hope of his asserting his individuality in society and therefore no possibility of social heroism in the novel. The man remains anonymous, obscure and insignificant, walking to his clerical desk in the early morning, strolling behind buildings during the lunch-hour and slipping quietly into his bed in the middle of the night when he is on shift duty. He is despised by his family and ignored by the world. He is a modern man who has been turned into a slave of bureaucracy.

*Camus, A., *L'Etranger*, Gallimard, Paris, 1942.

> The job was a filing job, and he had discovered that there were only about thirty letters a day needing to be put away, most probably never to be looked at again in one human life when one file was completed. (p. 155)

To this morally disarming knowledge that his life is being spent on the repetitive and insignificant business of carefully putting away useless letters is added the boredom and the emptiness of compulsory idling because there is only enough work for about three quarters of an hour each day. He has to accept his condition mutely and at the end is able to come to terms with the shrinking of human possibilities within the system. Men like Koomson discover that the desire for greatness which drives them is self-destructive. They are 'mimic men' who wallow in an imaginary sense of power and apprehend the reality when it is too late.

Duodu's *The Gab Boys*

Nkrumah's Ghana has also been used as the social setting of Cameron Duodu's novel, *The Gab Boys.** Unlike Armah who sees the plight of Ghana in the perspective of historical and social problems inter-related with man's selfish nature, Duodu interprets the situation mainly in terms of the selfishness and ineptitude of the leaders, and so the novel becomes a direct attack on Nkrumah's regime. Like Armah's novel, *The Gab Boys* adopts the tone of righteous anger towards that regime. However, this novel lacks artistic discipline and, far from ending on a pessimistic but questioning note, *The Gab Boys* concludes with an escape into a facile didacticism about the tribal past. After a comprehensively scathing criticism of a whole range of institutions of post-independence Ghana, the novel ends with two principal characters discussing the 'messages' of traditional drums which speak of a more democratic and more liberal past. Yet nothing is said about this past except that it existed: it is not clear how the author thinks it could benefit the present.

This novel too conjures up a nightmare situation. There is a sense of despair in the final conversation between the hero, Kwasa Asamoa and his bride-to-be, affectionately referred to as 'B'. She grumbles bitterly:

> And if, while Nkrumah is alive, you were to mention the names of past politicians, and even go so far as to call on them for help:

*Duodu, Cameron, *The Gab Boys*, André Deutsch, London, 1967.

> WE CAN'T SLEEP
> AND WE CALL YOU . . . .
>
> thus implying that he is not able to make you feel safe enough to sleep soundly, would he look on it with favour? (p. 206)

The experience which the hero has to go through in Accra is very close to a nightmare from which he escapes through a lucky marriage to return to Pusupusu, his native village. But the return is not altogether a happy one, for Asamoa comes home chiefly for the burial of one of his best friends, who has been killed in a motor accident. It is the burial atmosphere which moves the village elders to an act of mercy and enables them to forget Asamoa's past guilt.

The story centres on the fortunes of a single character who is also the narrator. He is a young school-leaver who finds himself among the underprivileged members of the community, whom the government does not seem to care for. He joins a group of other unemployed adolescents who spend all their time idling about the village. They go round smashing bottles on shop verandas, burning the sheds of market women, harassing passing girls and indulging in gratuitous provocation. These activities culminate in a senseless attack on an innocent shopkeeper, simply because he does not belong to their tribe. This focuses the attention of the village elders on the dangerous gang of adolescents who are then rounded up for their failure to pay tax. Most of them escape to Accra where they try to find employment. The hero's subsequent efforts to find a decent livelihood affords him an insight into the social realities of his country. He awakens to the fact that he has been condemned, along with many of his contemporaries, to lead a life of hardship, idleness and want because they have been born in an underprivileged class from which it is impossible to escape. The 'intelligentsia' who are in power have allocated all social privileges to themselves and closed the doors to further entry into their class. The only way to get a job is to know someone in the establishment, or else to have enough money to buy your way in.

Much of the social criticism in the novel centres on the educational set-up of the country which inculcates into its youth values which breed unrealizable aspirations within the society. There is no organized means by which the numerous school-leavers who cannot gain entrance to higher education institutions can be absorbed in the public sector. And yet all of them, as a result of their education, have grown to despise working with their hands. The cliché-appeals of the politicians for the school-leavers to return to the land fall on deaf ears. Every person who has been to school expects to find a white-collar job, but of course there are not enough to go round. This is the recurrent situation in many developing countries where educational facilities have been greatly expanded while the economies of the countries have remained relatively static, or have not expanded sufficiently to cope with the increased demand for employment which arises from increased manpower output from the educational institutions. The inevitable drift into the city for most of these young people ends with many of them sooner or later turning to a life of crime.

But it is not the educational set-up as such which the novel finds fault with; it is the whole philosophy behind the education policy and the general direction which the country is taking. A school system which produces a lot of young people with a little textbook education, who do not fit into any of the country's manpower needs is ill-conceived. In this case the fault is that the school system has been imported in a finished form from Europe. It is not related to the social needs of the country. Worse still the academic education which the young people receive awakens them to the inadequacies of the social system.

> We Gab Boys of Pusupusu knew that 'corruption' and 'nepotism' meant that the ideal goal of our society was far from being achieved, so we resigned ourselves to being *UNBEEZ*. . . . (p. 28)

By teaching social goals which the political system negates, the regime is undermining its own stability. It is this contradiction which underlies the frustration and meaningless misdemeanors of the Gab Boys.

The novel suffers from an overdose of political didacticism. No incident is allowed to pass without serving as an occasion for direct comment on the political problems of Ghana. When the narrator describes the lawless activities of the Gab Boys he adds:

> It was such 'adventures' that made life worth living for us. For to be quite frank, we had nothing else to live for. We respected nothing and nobody, and in turn, no one respected us or cared two hoots about us. There we were, none older than twenty, a whole pack of lads, our imaginations fuelled to combustion point by the many action-packed American films we saw each time we took a trip to a big town. And yet we had no creative occupation to provide an outlet for the hot zeal within us. We had all 'finished' school, and yet we had no work. (p. 25)

This is the kind of comment which tends to bore the reader because it is stating what he already knows, as if the author was trying to make sure that we do not interpret the situation in any other way than he intends us to. This pre-occupation with instructing the reader about the social realities of Ghana makes the author, masquerading behind a naive narrator, expound the problems he considers important rather than allow them to emerge from the story as live, problematical situations. The narrator is crudely manipulated to the extent that he lacks individuality. One moment he is the naive adolescent, talking about himself with self-pity, excusing all the folly which he and his colleagues commit:

> So they shouldn't look on us only from the outside and conclude that we were a pack of blokes who wanted to be idle and nothing more. Had anybody reported anything missing in the village which had been traced to us? I asked them. Had we taken anybody's wife? Nothing of the sort had happened, which showed that deep down, we were sweeter than angels, in spite of our outward show of tough-guy manners. (p. 19)

Another moment, as in the earlier quotation, he is saying that 'to be frank' they were a nuisance in the village. One moment he is rationalizing his failure to pass examinations by putting all the blame on the system, another moment he is saying that the corrupt system is to the advantage of the Gab Boys because they could not pass even if they were given a fair opportunity to compete:

> For we knew perfectly well that if bribery were uprooted and we were offered a fair chance to compete in examinations for entry into the clerical jobs we longed for, few of us could ever make a good enough grade. (p. 28)

There is a lack of consistency in the way the narrator attempts to examine himself. Had the contradictions been skilfully handled, we might have seen them as aspects of the narrator's character. However, they are often left to appear more like authorial inconsistency. But the contradictory views of the main character are also made to reflect on his lack of self-awareness. Right up to the end, Kwasa Asamoa convinces himself that the girl whom he is in love with and whom he affectionately calls 'B' is innocent, although he knows very well that for a long time she has been a kept girl. This unwillingness on the part of the narrator to face any painful truth makes us distrust him, even when he 'confesses'. We never know which aspect of him to take seriously. His views and reactions are essentially trivial and this is best exemplified in his final 'confession' that he does not love 'B' after all, that all the time he has been wanting to sleep with her as a means of avenging himself on her class:

> In fact, to be quite frank, even B herself, whom I loved so much, had been a victim of my self-pity; while making love to her, I'd partly been avenging myself on her class. Was that what proper love should be? She had enjoyed the fruit of my vengeance, no doubt, but if she knew what I'd been saying in my head, it would have revolted her. (p. 165)

If this admission was to be taken seriously as the narrator's secret motive then we would not expect him to get married to 'B'. Right through the novel the narrator employs the phrase 'to be frank' to introduce explanations which contradict what he has said before. But his 'frankness' often amounts to nothing more than petty remarks which are no less self-deluding than what he has said previously. He does not offer us any keen insights into the complex situation and up to the end he is still rationalizing his motives:

> Every society in which there is injustice produces such warped relations; those hard judged by the ill-treated are often just unwitting participants of the injustice; but they suffer ill-will all the same. (p. 165)

This is the explanation which he invents to explain the falsity of his relationship with 'B'. Since Asamoa confesses that he is not in love with her their marriage gives us no sense of fulfilment. He simply uses her to get into a higher economic class, the class which he spends so much time attacking.

Duodu presents a young man struggling to find a secure position in society which offers him no opportunity to criticize the class which is generally referred to in the novel as 'the intelligentsia'. Members of this class are often described in sarcastic terms and with an implied moral superiority on the part of the narrator. Every meeting and every incident in the novel serves as an occasion for the narrator to protest against what he regards as an exploiting class. The description of the official of the railways who helps Asamoa to find a job serves as a good illustration of the cultivated superiority which the narrator takes towards those who appear to him to be privileged:

> The friend was not so large as Mr Aryee but he too had a slightly bulging stomach and puffed cheeks; the trade marks of the new rulers of Ghana, at the lower level. They were people who had attended secondary school at the time the British were here, when to go to secondary school was a very great achievement because there were not more than ten secondary schools in a country of over five million people. Many of them had later got scholarships to study abroad and had come back to occupy big positions made available by the government's Africanization programme. . . . They had bungalows and cars and good salaries—just as the white men who created their jobs did. And they were downright 'honest'—they knew that if you got a job from them you would receive money, so hell, you ought to give them money to get you a job, even if you were qualified for it. (p. 125)

While many novels which describe the corruption and moral decadence of the post-independence era tend to single out politicians for attack, this novel accuses indiscriminately all those who hold important positions in society, whether they are politicians, civil servants or business men. And when it attacks politicians it does not leave out members of the opposition. They are all selfish and corrupt, doing the things which they commonly denounce on public platforms. About ministers the narrator says:

> Ministers went onto platform after platform denouncing bribery and corruption, nepotism and favouritism. Yet no sooner did they get a call on their 'direct' line than they were onto the principal secretary: 'Is that the P.S.? Oh, this is the minister. Don't mention—it was due to you. Now, P.S., you've got to help me out . . . yes, again; you know how helpful they are in one's constituency and yet how embarrassing they can be when they come to Accra . . . .' (p. 126)

And then he adds a comment on the civil servants:

> And the lovers of theory think that the Principal or Permanent Secretaries and their Assistant Secretaries ensure 'continuity' in government policy because they can tell their Ministers, who may be new, what is 'departmental practice' and what is not. Hahahahaha! (p. 126)

The group of junior civil servants who meet frequently in Mr Aryee's house are used to illustrate the privileges of their class. They often indulge in shoddy political discussions as they drink ice-cold beer and dance with young girls who try to use their sex to push themselves higher on the social scale. They discuss the problems of the country without any real concern because their positions are secure. This contrasts sharply with the manner in which political discussions are conducted in the villages, where politics often serves as an outlet for people's frustrations. Violence often accompanies political campaigns because the masses have been incited by the politicians to vent their anger against imaginary enemies—either members of other tribes or other political groups—while the real enemy is the privileged élite. Sometimes the author abandons the story and gives a catalogue of privileges, the narrating voice often taking on the same uncritical bitterness which we have already met with in Ayi Kwei Armah.

> And just as the people who actually sleep with lovely actresses don't wake up exhausted but refreshed, so the real inheritors of Ghana's goods were driving past us in comfortable cars even as we were dragging our weary flesh home. They would go home and sink into comfortable chairs and drink champagne while nestling into the arms of lovely, soft women. And while they drank, we would suffer the hangover. The drink would open their minds to better ways of sitting comfortably and nestling into the arms of prettier, more scintillating women. And their houses would become bigger as the women gave rein to their vain imaginings; marble would be imported from Michelangelo's country to make floors, but asses who didn't know the true use of marble would, having heard of drapings, relegate it to a monstrous undergrowth, covering it with deep, squelching carpets into which would sink very high heels manufactured in Italy, France and Switzerland. (p. 144)

In this uncontrolled outburst against the system the narrator assumes the role of a spokesman for the underprivileged. He classifies himself with the 'low people'. The descriptions of the hardships of these 'low people' has the same quality of sentimental exaggeration as we find in the catalogues of privilege, as we are implored to see nothing but grotesque opulence on one hand and lamentable deprivation on the other. At one point Kwasa Asamoa describes himself working on a farm with his father for little reward and labours his point with an explicit comment:

> It was thousands of hard-working men like that who cultivated the cocoa which produces sixty per cent of Ghana's national income. And men, some of whom had never known what it was to slip downhill on a wet morning with a full load of cocoa on one's head, decided how much to give them and how much to keep in the state coffers from which they filched millions to build castles both on the ground and in the air. The poor old men used most of their money paying cut-throat prices to drug peddlers for medicine to sustain their protein-starved bodies. And the flatulent nincompoops in Accra and Kumasi drank away and talked and laughed. (pp. 153–4)

This indignant, abusive language does not tell us anything about the peculiar problems of Ghana. It is too melodramatic. The novel is at its best when the narrator's speech assumes a simple, oral character, relying on colloquialisms to capture the mood of the young man who, though distressed, finds enough leisure to be puzzled and fascinated by the city. But when he abandons this simple style to launch a bitter attack on Nkrumah's regime we get the impression that he is being used as a mouthpiece for the author's opinions. We do not see any members of the government as individual beings responding to complex situations. We only hear loud denunciations of their activities from an enraged, rather irresponsible and dishonest young man. *The Gab Boys*, like many post-independence novels, conveys a sense of resentment against the way in which pre-independence ambitions have been betrayed by those to whom power has been entrusted. The narrator looks back with complete disillusionment and describes the events of independence as if they had been a mockery of the people's aspirations. Describing Nkrumah's behaviour on independence day the narrator says:

> After he had duly shouted, he talked a lot about 'coming battles' and things like that, and then suddenly, there was an electrifying change in his voice and he shouted at the top of his voice, as if his own sexual excitement had reached its peak:
> 'OUR INDEPENDENCE IS MEANINGLESS UNLESS IT IS LINKED UP WITH THE TOTAL LIBERATION OF THE WHOLE AFRICAN CONTINENT!'
> The sharpness of his voice, the intensity with which he said this, communicated itself to the crowd and before his voice had died down there was such a loud yell that if I wanted to reproduce it faithfully, I'd have to let it go for at least five pages. Which, of course, is a waste of paper. (p. 143)

However, the author's choice of an angry, jobless narrator who tries to see all his problems as the result of exploitation by the privileged class becomes a severe limitation on the novel. What we get is a strictly narrow view of a self-pitying young man who is mainly telling a story about himself but indulges in laboured digressions about the inefficacy of the political system that has produced him.

The sentimental relationship between Asamoa and 'B' ends in a betrothal. The return of a rebel to the village after much fruitless wandering in the city is used as a motif to produce the *dénouément*. The occasion of Asamoa's return is a mixture of laughter and sorrow, for he comes back with the dead body of one of the young men of the village who has been killed through exposure to the menace of the city. The mourning brings a feeling of remorse which makes the village chief forgive Asamoa for his past misconduct. The hero's return to his native village after an excruciating sojourn in the city gives him a heightened understanding of the beauty of his own traditions and the significance of the past. In the final scene 'B' is instructing him about the great wisdom which lies in the poetry, music and the sayings of the tribe. She tells him:

> Technology does not teach ideals; our ideals are our love of freedom, our love of music and dancing and our concern for each other's welfare, which we show through the responsibility we assume for hordes of people in what is called our 'extended families'. Those are the important things; technology will be acquired anyhow—even monkeys can be taught to drive cars. (pp. 207–8)

Until this last conversation in the novel, technology has not been mentioned and the social problems which are described stem from other causes. This sudden dismissal of technology and defensive assertion of the value of traditional ways of tribal living is an obtrusive cliché. The hero finds a temporary escape into drums and dance but the problems which the novel has stated are not going to be dissolved away by dancing and the recital of traditional proverbs. The hero embraces the past only because he wishes to escape from the necessary process of coming to terms with the present.

The Beautyful Ones Are Not Yet Born and *The Gab Boys* reflect another shift in the changing mood of the African novel. In the novels discussed in Chapter 4 under the heading of 'Disenchantment', corruption, nepotism, materialism and political ineptitude are denounced but we meet heroes who still believe that the course of society can be changed, and that order can be restored. This faith in the underlying values of society inspires the heroes to political action which often results in an important gesture being made so that society can awaken from the malaise into which it has allowed itself to sink. But in the last class of novels such a gesture is no longer possible. The individual can only assert his own values by opting out of the social system which denies him self-realization. He no longer has the power to change his society; all he can do is find for himself a corner where he can shelter from the nightmare.

NOTES

1. Howe, Irving, *Politics and the Novel*, Horizon Press, New York, 1957, p. 235.
2. Noble, R. W., 'A Beautiful Novel', *Journal of Commonwealth Literature*, no. 9, London, July 1970, p. 117.
3. Jones, Eldred, 'The Beautyful Ones Are Not Yet Born', *African Literature Today*, no. 3, London, 1968, p. 56.
4. Kariara, J., 'The Beautyful Ones Are Not Yet Born', *Zuka*, no. 4, Nairobi, December 1969, p. 57.
5. Nkrumah, Kwame, *The Class Struggle in Africa*, Panaf Books, London, 1970.
6. Okara, Gabriel, *The Voice*, African Writers Series, Heinemann Educational Books Ltd, London, 1970 (1964).
7. Naipaul, V. S., *The Mimic Men*, André Deutsch, London, 1967.
8. Povey, John, 'The Beautyful Ones Are Not Yet Born', *Africa Report*, Washington, February 1969, p. 60.

6. Commitment

Ngugi's *A Grain of Wheat*

In their fictional interpretation of history African novelists have been involved in the search for ways of combating the forces of disintegration that have been let loose by unhappy circumstances of history. Many have looked into the past to see whether it has any lessons to offer the present. Others have been content with depicting the truth about the present but in so doing have tended to present societies that are sick because they have lost the internal dynamic to resist the infiltration of evil. The committed novel, on the other hand, necessarily looks into the future because of implied faith in the ability of a people to change their history. Sembene Ousmane and Ngugi share this faith in the ability of their societies to hold their own against evil and to unite in the struggle towards a desirable social ideal.

Two of the first three published novels by Ngugi are concerned with the Mau Mau revolt by the Kikuyu against the British administration in Kenya in the fifties. Ngugi's novels are 'committed' in the sense that colonialism is the constant object of attack. The author-narrator is entirely on the side of revolt, stressing the atrocities of the colonial administration and the heroism of the forest rebels who are fighting against colonial domination. However, the author does not idealize the rebels. In *Weep Not, Child*,[1] death and suffering result from the jealousy and hatred which exist between three neighbouring families. The Mau Mau crisis only serves to bring age-old hostilities to the surface. At the outbreak of violence the people are unwilling to risk their security by taking part in the war of liberation. *A Grain of Wheat** deals more directly with the events of the war. But while the liberation struggle is successful the attainment of independence brings to the society the rather disquieting knowledge of its own weaknesses.

The general tone of *A Grain of Wheat* is one of bitterness and anger. The painful memories of Mau Mau violence still overhang the Kikuyu villages

*Ngugi, *A Grain of Wheat*, African Writers Series, Heinemann Educational Books Ltd, London, 1968 (1967). (Page references are to the reset 1975 edition.)

as the attainment of independence fails to bring the cherished social dreams. The celebrations of Uhuru break up in confusion and disappointment. Everything in the novel gravitates around this central event, the celebration of independence. All the events in the novel have been directly or indirectly related to the struggle for independence and therefore, understandably, the celebration of this event becomes the symbolic focus of the people's aspirations and social dreams. All celebrations are symbolic because they enable participants to express unequal and varied emotions through a common and often simple gesture. The imagination lends elasticity to the simple gesture so that it assumes all the dimensions of the larger event which is being celebrated. Ngugi employs this symbolic relationship between the simple ritual and the larger event to explore the sentiments and anxieties of the villagers of Rungei towards the birth of the Kenyan nation on the day of independence. Far from being an occasion for jubilation the ceremony uncovers the unpleasant realities which the community has so far been unwilling to face. Thus by carefully structuring the novel around this momentous event in the history of the nation the author is able to highlight the illusions which tend to be fostered by the euphoric atmosphere of independence.

A Grain of Wheat comes close to being a historical novel. Its plot owes almost everything to the violent events of the Mau Mau movement. In many ways the novel is a defence of that movement. It is a creative interpretation of national history in a favourable light. It celebrates national heroes who fought for a national cause although it does so without idealizing them. In a different way it fulfils the same function as the autobiographical accounts of the ex-Mau Mau fighters. In one of the best known of these, *Mau Mau Detainee*[2] the author, Josiah Mwangi Kariuki, defends the movement in which he was involved against colonial charges that it was a movement of blood rituals and murderous atrocities. Some of the incidents which are described in the account have their parallel in Ngugi's novel. Tom Mboya's *Freedom and After*[3] is another defence of the same movement. But while Mboya's concern is with the political aspects of the movement, and Kariuki is interested in rendering an accurate account of what went on in colonial detention camps, Ngugi uses the events to portray the emotional tensions and private suffering which the violence caused to the community. What all these works have in common is that they celebrate the same national heroes who fought for independence and put the blame for the violence on those who opposed the freedom struggle. All these works are part of the same historical process of a re-assessment of their moral position by a people during their struggle against foreign rule. As Professor Mazrui (himself a Kenyan) has written:

> Next to forgetting past enemies, the most important element in building up a national consciousness is perhaps the faculty of remembering past heroes. This involves recognizing the heroes as common heroes. And this act of recognition itself is an exercise in national self-identification. To put it another way, the idea of a nation can sometimes be a little too abstract, and hence a little too cold, to command ready human allegiance. To give the idea of a nation warmth, it is often necessary either to personify it metaphorically, or, more effectively, to give it specific human form in national heroes.[4]

The cult of heroes is an important phenomenon in the newly independent countries of Africa and recurs again and again as a theme in many novels, especially those written in the last decade. This theme is given an important place in *A Grain of Wheat*. Mugo, the man chosen for crowning as hero on the day of independence, turns out to be the man who betrayed the leader of the forest fighters. Karanja, the man who has been condemned by public opinion and who is to be publicly humiliated at the ceremony, turns out to be innocent. Through this dramatic irony, Ngugi warns his society against an over-hasty process of setting up heroes to worship and traitors to persecute.

While the novel speaks against the harshness of colonial oppression, it is equally bitter against the new leaders of Kenya who are neglecting the interests of the peasant masses who were the people who made the greatest sacrifices during the war of liberation. Ngugi speaks on behalf of those who, in his view, have been neglected by the new government. Those who took shelter in institutions such as universities and government service and safely avoided having to fight for independence are the ones who take the greatest rewards when freedom is won. Gikonyo laments aloud to Mugo:

> 'It is people like you who ought to have been the first to taste the fruits of independence. But now, whom do we see riding in long cars and changing them daily as if motor cars were clothes? It is those who did not take part in the movement, the same who ran to the shelter of schools and universities and administration. At political meetings you hear them shout: Uhuru, Uhuru, we fought for. Fought where? They were uncircumcised boys. They knew suffering as a word.' (pp. 60–1)

The passage has its ambivalence. It is, of course, an indictment of the political élite which is appropriating privilege to itself while the people who bore the burden of the liberation struggle remain deprived. But there is an underlying irony in the passage: the man who is being praised for his heroism in the struggle is the traitor who betrayed the leading Mau Mau fighter, Kihika, to the colonial administration.

As we have already observed in earlier chapters, many recent novelists from West as well as East Africa have voiced concern for the greed of African élites and their disregard of the interests of the peasant masses. It is significant to note that while most other novelists write from a detached position Ngugi identifies himself entirely with the masses. At least in four separate instances the author uses the pronoun 'we'. The reader is meant to see the author-narrator as a member of the class on whose behalf he is speaking. Ngugi also has the special distinction of drawing all his main characters from the peasant class. This however, tends to impose certain limitations upon the novel. The characters are too simple and too inarticulate to provide us with a full understanding of the complexities of national politics. The reader gets a discomforting impression that the events of the novel have a much wider significance than can be grasped in the interactions of peasant characters. Sometimes the author tries to overcome this by attributing to his characters a greater social awareness than is convincing, for instance when at their local meetings they discuss Gandhi and Indian politics and the American War of Independence.

As a writer, Ngugi constantly shows his preoccupation with the plight of the peasant masses. He has castigated fellow African writers who ignore the importance of this class. He writes about Soyinka as follows:

> Soyinka's good man is the uncorrupted individual. His liberal humanism leads him to admire an individual's lone act of courage, and thus often he ignores the creative struggle of the masses. The ordinary people, the workers and peasants, in his plays remain passive watchers on the shore or pitiful comedians on the road.[5]

Elsewhere he has lamented the failure of African writers to portray the basic realities of modern African societies. Speaking of the reality which they must write about he says:

> . . . the basic reality in Africa is that 80 per cent of the people live below the bread-line standard. . . .[6]

He goes on:

> When we, the black intellectuals, the black bourgeoisie, got the power, we never tried to bring about the policies which would be in harmony with the needs of the 80 per cent of peasants and workers. I think that it is high time African writers also started to talk in terms of these workers and peasants.

Ngugi then may be seen as a novelist of the people—trying to express their suffering and their aspirations from within. This sometimes makes him idealize their moral fortitude, their physical endurance and their selflessness. On the whole the African novel has tended to portray the masses as a passive class on whom history is made by the political and the military élite. On occasions the masses may participate in rallies and riots but they generally do so without any understanding of the issues involved. This is clearly the case in many novels discussed in earlier chapters.

The clash between the Kikuyu community and the white settlers appears essentially economic. It starts when the settlers begin to acquire land and does not end until the invader has been defeated. But the supreme importance which the Kikuyu attach to their land has been described by Jomo Kenyatta in his anthropological treatise, *Facing Mount Kenya*, where implications go beyond the merely economic:

> As agriculturalists the Gikuyu people depend entirely on the land. It supplies them with the material needs of life, through which mental and spiritual contentment is achieved. Communion with the ancestral spirits is perpetuated through contact with the soil in which the ancestors of the tribe lie buried. The Gikuyu consider the earth as the 'mother' of the tribe, for the reason that the mother bears her burden for about eight to nine moons while the child is in her womb, and then for a short period of suckling. But it is the soil that feeds the child through a lifetime; and again after death it is the soil that nurses the spirit of the dead for eternity. Thus the earth is the most sacred thing above all that dwell in or on it. Among the Gikuyu the soil is especially honoured, and an everlasting oath is to swear by the earth.[7]

It is against this background that the conflict takes place. Land is not simply an economic commodity, it is the custodian of the most sacred objects of the tribe. The ejection of the Kikuyu from their land therefore at once signifies material deprivation as well as an attack on the traditional way of life. Kihika, the leading fighter in *A Grain of Wheat*, explains to his colleague, Wambuku, the true meaning of the conflict:

> It is not politics, Wambuku . . . it is life. Is he a man who lets another take away his land and freedom, has a slave life? (p. 85)

It is for this that the Kikuyu are prepared to sacrifice their lives to win back their land. The oath of allegiance to the Kikuyu Central Association which came to be associated with the Mau Mau was administered with a Bible in the left hand and soil in the right hand.[8]

The nature of this oath brings us to another major theme in the novel, namely the way Christian religion is interpreted to serve the interests of the revolutionary movement. Land serves as the motive for revolt while Christianity provides the moral force. Resistance first takes root in the missionary centres. Christian converts are taught that they are the children of God and they begin to look for their own black Moses to deliver them from colonial servitude.

> Meanwhile, the missionary centres hatched new leaders; they refused to eat the good things of Pharaoh: instead, they chose to cut grass and make bricks with the other children. (p. 13)

Thus the colonialist's own teaching is turned against him. Kihika, the leader of the freedom fighters finds his chief inspiration from the Bible, which he always carries along with him wherever he goes. Among the lines which Kihika underlines in red in his personal Bible are, significantly, the same lines that have attracted American negro composers of folk songs:

> And the Lord spoke unto Moses,
> Go unto Pharaoh, and say unto him,
> Thus sayeth the Lord,
> Let my people go.

Kihika sees himself as the chosen instrument of God to deliver the Kikuyu from colonial bondage. The Kikuyu peasants erect themselves into 'the chosen people' of God. This bizarre interpretation of the scriptures can be explained in terms of East African evangelism in which foreign religions are often seized with great enthusiasm and re-interpreted to suit the people's own aspirations. Georges Balandier has commented on this phenomenon:

> One of the most characteristic phenomenon of sociocultural change occuring during the colonial period in numerous societies in christianized Black Africa is the appearance of messianistic movements which gave rise to more or less ephemeral NEGRO CHURCHES. Although they are outwardly religious, these movements rapidly develop a political aspect. They are at the origin of nationalisms which are still unsophisticated but unequivocal in their expression.[9]

The re-interpretation of the Bible in this manner by the Kikuyu had already been treated by Ngugi in his first novel, *Weep Not, Child.* The periods covered by the two novels overlap and the social background to both is very much the same. The social processes which are described in *Weep Not, Child* help us to understand better the events of *A Grain of Wheat.* The young boy, Njoroge, growing up in Kenya just before the Emergency and subjected to the oppression and deprivation which was the lot of his countrymen, and equally subjected to a strong dose of Christian teaching, begins to equate the situation of his people with that of the children of Israel during their captivity in Egypt. When Kenyatta calls upon them to rebel against their condition they set him up as their black Moses.

Ngugi then sees the colonialist's religion turned into a weapon against him. The Kikuyu notice the contradiction between the white man's teachings and his behaviour. They reject his actions but embrace his creed.

They also discover a close similarity between their traditional religion and the new teaching. The myth of Gikuyu and Mumbi has close similarities with the Christian myth of Adam and Eve and as far as the young Njoroge is concerned it is the same myth.

Apart from religion there is another strong moral force which sustains the Kikuyu in their revolt, namely their awareness that they are part of a world-wide struggle against oppression and imperialist domination. True there are those among them who believe that the white man cannot be conquered. Karanja says to Kihika:

> 'What can we do? . . . They have got the guns and the bombs. See how they whipped Hitler.' (p. 77)

But Kihika rejects this kind of defeatism and replies:

> 'It's a question of Unity. The example of India is there before our noses. The British were there for hundreds and hundreds of years. They ate India's wealth. They drank India's blood. They never listened to the political talk-talk of a few men. What happened? There came this man Gandhi. Mark you, Gandhi knows his whiteman well. He goes round and organizes the Indian masses into a weapon stronger than the bomb.' (p. 77)

These views reflect what has often been said by many nationalist leaders. Namely, that the Second World War and the independence of India were powerful influences on their own fight for freedom. If other countries could resist domination by the Nazis and if India could resist British domination, so could African countries; so their reasoning went. The interpretation of the Mau Mau struggle by James Ngugi suggests that even the peasants in Kenya were becoming aware of what was going on in the rest of the world, particularly since many had served in the war or knew those who had served. In the detention camps, Gatu, the former oath administrator of Nyeri, comforts his fellow detainees by telling them about the imprisonment of Gandhi and Nehru, the American war of independence and Napolcon. They see themselves as part of a world-wide movement which is destined to triumph. They see history as being on their side in the struggle and this strengthens their will to fight. Their leaders also point out, among other things, that black people lost their lives in defending Britain against Nazi Germany. If they can fight to save another country from foreign domination they can fight to save themselves from the same evil.

The political conflict in the novel is polarized along racial lines. The Kikuyu see their suffering to be a direct result of the privileged position of the white settler community, the marginal profits being collected by the

Asian traders. The image of the white man in Ngugi's novels is fairly representative of what we commonly find in African fiction. The white man—especially the colonial administrator—is often portrayed as a narrow-minded, brutal debauchee, selfish and ruthless in his dealings with natives and cunning and dishonest in his dealings with his fellow white men. This view of the European emerges most clearly in the West African French novel. Ferdinand Oyono, Mongo Beti and Sembene Ousmane tend to adopt a certain superiority towards this kind of European because he is deficient in humanity. Ngugi's Englishmen are less of caricatures but the relationships and attitudes of the white man towards the blacks follow this pattern. John Thompson is ruled by the paranoia of turning the British Empire into a great moral idea. This obsession blinds him to many realities which surround him in the strife-torn society of Kenya. His studies of history and philosophy at Oxford have only served him by providing him with a wider source of facts to rationalize his narrow-minded conception. The notes which he collects for his intended volume, *Prospero in Africa*, are a mass of the second-rate and the cliché. Thompson makes entries such these:

> *Dr Albert Schweitzer says 'the Negro is a child, and with children, nothing can be done without the use of authority.' I've now worked in Nyeri, Githima, Kisumu, Ngong. I agree.*
>
> *In dealing with the African you are often compelled to do the unexpected. A man came into my office yesterday. He told me about a wanted terrorist leader. From the beginning, I was convinced the man was lying, was really acting, perhaps to trap me or hide his own part in the movement. He seemed to be laughing at me. Remember the African is a born actor, that's why he finds it so easy to lie. Suddenly I spat into his face, I don't know why, but I did it.* (pp. 49–50)

John Thompson is an ardent believer in the civilizing mission of colonialism. He wants to extend the French policy of assimilation to embrace the masses of the colonized people and yet in his life as a member of the exclusive colonial community he practises the kind of discrimination that makes useful contact between the two races impossible. But he does not realize the contradiction between his benevolent sentiments and his behaviour: he is too narrow-minded. His naive loyalty to the imperialist cause takes on egregious qualities through the excessive emotions which well up in him when he sees Princess Elizabeth during her visit to Kenya.

> He was then District Officer. He felt a thrill: his heart-beat had quickened almost as if a covenant had been made between him and her. Then, there, he would have done anything for her, would have stabbed himself

> to prove his readiness to carry out that mission which though unspoken seemed embodied in her person and smile. (pp. 37–8)

This exaggerated loyalty may sound a little unreal even for a crusader of colonialism if he happens to be as educated as Thompson is unless we acknowledge the superficiality of his emotional education. When Britain decides to grant independence to Kenya he feels betrayed and tenders his resignation so that he may be saved from the humiliation of serving under African leaders.

It is this narrow-minded John Thompson whom we are told is the most progressive of the colonial service community in Nairobi. The rest live in an even narrower world of prejudices. Thompson's own wife offers her first cup of tea to an African a few days before her departure from the country. And she does so completely out of curiosity because the talk of independence makes her begin to wonder about the human qualities of the African. The only things she will miss about Africa are the sunshine and the cheap labour. Her feelings are shared by most of the colonial service community who as a rule disguise their attachment to the physical comfort which Africa offers them as a commitment to the service against communism. Besides, they are all afraid of going back to their own country because they doubt their own ability to stand up to the competition of that society. Their coming to Africa has been partly a desire to escape from self-recognition, and to find illusory compensations for their frustrated self-importance.

Just as the villagers of Rungei are trying to crown a martyr to their struggle for freedom so the colonial officials are looking for their own martyr. They also see themselves as sufferers, betrayed by their own government and having to leave behind everything they have worked for for so long.

> Thompson's imminent departure and the Independence tomorrow night brought back in their hearts the man who had been at the centre of scandal at Rira. Thompson was therefore a martyr, had been so received at Githima, was so regarded now on the eve of his departure from a country he had served so well. (p. 142)

It is the turn for the European community to live in fear and anxiety, to feel harassed and insecure.

Racial tension does not play the important role which it often plays in South African novels, or even in the novels from French Africa. Nevertheless we are constantly aware of it as a vital factor which has a catalytic effect upon a conflict which is primarily political and economic. Although the Kikuyu define their struggle as a struggle for land and freedom sometimes their definition takes on racial overtones. In *Weep Not, Child* an address by one of the Kikuyu leaders to his supporters is reported in this manner.

> All the land belonged to the people—black people. They had been given it by God. For every race had their country. The Indians had India. Europeans had Europe. And Africans had Africa, the land of the black people (applause). (p. 64)

Racial tension is played down in the novel and is only seen as a part of the political conflict; but there is no suggestion that the resolution of the main conflict has settled the issue of racial hostility. On the eve of independence the colonial officials are still determined to cling to the last particle of privilege. Thompson's last words are: 'We are not yet beaten. Africa cannot, cannot do without Europe' (p. 144). Thus the conflict is about to assume a different aspect.

Derek Elders has complained that the European characters in the novel are two-dimensional.[10] This is unfair to Ngugi because these characters are not simply villains. We see them as individuals who have been caught in a social conflict which extends beyond their lives. This is not to deny, however, that the characters have a certain flatness. Nor is this limited to white characters. Many of the black characters remain mere symbols of suffering. Ngugi always gives the reader a clear general picture of community life around the villages in which his novels are set, but his individual characters are often weak. In *A Grain of Wheat* we get a sharp impression of what social life must have been like in Kikuyu villages during the Mau Mau, but there are no deeply moving personalities in the novel. Only the relationship between Gikonyo and Mumbi grows sufficiently complex to bear the tragic sense which the author is trying to create. Mugo's muteness remains unfathomable. When his guilt is finally revealed we know that he has for long been burdened by it but the depth of his suffering can only be guessed at because it is never fully communicated. Less disciplined novelists such as Cyprian Ekwensi and T. M. Aluko have created more moving personalities. The problem seems to be that Ngugi has not yet been able to create a character of sufficiently sustained complexity to support the weight of his complex public themes. In *Weep Not, Child* there is a half successful attempt to load such a complex theme upon a simple story of growing up. The novel is essentially about Njoroge's childhood during the period preceding the Mau Mau and the early days of that movement. It is also about a sentimental love relationship between the young Kikuyu boy, Njoroge and a young Kikuyu girl, Mwihaki. *The River Between*, again a fairly simple plot of a religious conflict between the people of two opposite ridges, is overburdened with the attempt to deal with the more complex and public theme of the transition of a traditional community into modernity. In all these novels one becomes vaguely aware of passing events of great historical importance but the simple and limited characters are inadequate to lead us to an understanding of these events.

The author's note at the beginning of *A Grain of Wheat* states the problem he is trying to convey. 'But the situation and the problems are real—sometimes too painfully real for the peasants who fought the British yet who now see all that they fought for being put on one side.' The village drama described in the novel barely touches on the main culprit of this betrayal namely, the government of Kenya. We only meet one Member of Parliament in the novel, and only very briefly, and there is no evidence to suggest that his behaviour reflects the general pattern of the relationship between the central government and the people. In fact, the national leader, Kenyatta, is idealized. The villagers are only disillusioned about a local hero of the Mau Mau fighting. But Mugo has nothing to do with the new government. There exists a gap between the plot and the political theme over which the structure of the novel strains and sometimes appears to be in danger of breaking.

The cumbersome narrative technique which the novel employs also produces a certain amount of slackness. The flash-back technique is a delicate one and must be used in such a way that the story is built up without leaving gaps that irritate and confuse the reader and interfere with the sense of continuity. Suspense, if not properly controlled, can reduce rather than increase the interest for the reader, and this sometimes happens in this novel. Our involvement in the central theme is over-delayed. In the early part of the novel we follow numerous episodes which give us disjointed views of the different characters without establishing their importance to the story. The first chapter introduces Mugo but before our interest has been sufficiently aroused in him the second chapter switches our attention by giving us an account of the resistance. In the next chapter we begin to sense the importance of Mugo but still nothing decisive happens. In fact Mugo does not emerge as an important character until well into the second half of the novel; meanwhile we follow the disjointed life histories of Karanja, Gikonyo, Mumbi, Thompson and a host of minor characters, yet their lives do not interrelate until the final chapters. This makes it difficult for the reader to gain a clear picture of the pattern of events.

Although the multiple nature of the plot reduces narrative strength, the orchestration of the common theme of betrayal in the parallel segments of the plot preserves thematic unity. Mugo betrays Kihika, the leader of the forest fighters. Gikonyo betrays the movement by breaking the oath. As a result of this betrayal he is freed from jail only to find that his wife has betrayed him by sleeping with another man. Karanja betrays his people by siding with the colonial establishment. Finally the newly elected Member of Parliament betrays the electorate and begins to use his position to amass wealth at the expense of the people who elected him. On the day of independence when Mugo confesses his guilt all these betrayals come into perspective and the people of Rungei are forced to re-examine their euphoristic regard for independence. But Ngugi seems to overplay the public importance of the disillusion. The most important thing about Mugo's confession is that it enables Gikonyo and Mumbi to recognize their cruelty towards each other. They have both been looking to Mugo as the exemplary man in the community. When they discover that he is the traitor of the community they are forced to re-examine their attitudes and to realize that men cannot be categorized into saints and villains. They conquer their own pride and forgive each other.

With regard to the political life of the country, however, the novel is less positive. The same gloomy atmosphere of the beginning remains at the end. Indeed there is a sadness in the novel which makes it almost an unrelieved chronicle of pain and suffering. It is this persistent dwelling on the suffering of the common people that has led Peter Nazareth to say:

> The realm of literary prophesy is a dangerous one, but I think that when Ngugi comes to write a novel dealing with problems of present-day Kenya, he will probably be committed to a kind of socialism.[11]

Whatever his ideological inclinations may be, the development of his art will depend on his ability to create characters with a capacity for life, and he will also have to explore points of view beyond his present range of peasant workers if he is to deal adequately with the major political themes that have been his persistent concern.

Ousmane's *God's Bits of Wood*

Most novels are written to illustrate an important truth about life which the author believes has never been acknowledged. But some novels go beyond this and try to champion a cause or principle which the author believes ought to prevail. Ousmane's *God's Bits of Wood** falls into this latter category. Ousmane's concern is with the dignity of man, especially as expressed through human labour. The life of the novel is informed by the author's faith that life ought to be a heroic struggle to defend the inalienable rights of all men to enjoy the fruits of their labour.

*Ousmane, Sembene, *God's Bits of Wood*, African Writers Series, Heinemann Educational Books Ltd, London, 1970 (1960). (Page references are to the reset 1976 edition.)

The novel shows an African society going through radical transformation as a result of a conflict between capital and labour. The plot revolves around this conflict and demonstrates the inevitable triumph of labour over capital. In this respect the novel is an attack on capitalism because of the way in which capitalism attempts to grade human beings on the basis of race, income, sex, age and various other bases that it relies on in order to undermine the potential solidarity of workers. Anything that tends to create gaps between men is evil because it undermines human dignity and therefore ought to be fought through collective effort. It is during the common struggle to defend this dignity that man's noblest qualities become manifest.

God's Bits of Wood is a social novel with a clear and loud social message. The expression of this message is the overriding aim to which everything else has been subordinated. No character is drawn with sufficient depth or complexity to make psychological exploration an important concern of the novel. No subtleties of symbolic suggestion are made to contribute to its meaning. The novel is dedicated to the recording of concrete facts about the working-class struggle, a struggle which gives the life of the workers new meaning and purpose.

God's Bits of Wood is an imaginative re-creation of a historical moment for the railway workers of former French West Africa. Between October 1947 and March 1948 these workers paralysed the railway services from Dakar to Niger by going on strike in defence of their right to enjoy the same social benefits as those enjoyed by white workers. The narrative is an imaginative account of what happened during the strike in three railway towns: Thies, Dakar and Bamako. Between these three main towns lie scores of settlements inhabited by thousands of Africans whose lives have become dependent upon the machine. Although it is they who maintain the railway services, they themselves depend upon the railway line for their livelihood. The novel explores this relationship of interdependence in order to illuminate the fundamental problems inherent in the conflict between labour and capital. When the workers go on strike they are revolting against being treated as slaves of industry and having their lives regulated by the machine; they are asserting their right to control the machine and to use it as an instrument of their own well-being.

> Every inhabitant of Thies, no matter who he was, depended on the railroad, and on the traffic between Koulikoro and Dakar. (p. 13)

This is the the ugly fact of dependence the workers have to face in their struggle to control the machine. When the strike is declared it sets in motion forces which bring about a completely new awareness:

> When the smoke from the trains no longer drifted above the savanna, they realized that an age had ended—an age their elders had told them about, when all of Africa was just a garden for food. Now the machine ruled over their lands, and when they forced every machine within a thousand miles to halt they became conscious of their strength, but conscious also of their dependence. They began to understand that the machine was making them a whole new breed of men. It did not belong to them; it was they who belonged to it. When it stopped, it taught them that lesson. (p. 32)

When sanctions are brought against the strikers and the whole community is threatened with starvation and haunted by the memory of the violence that accompanied the previous strike, the labourers, the housewives, the grandmothers, the schoolchildren—all realize that they are bound together in a new relationship with the machine. Even the destiny of the white workers has been brought close to that of the Africans by the machine. The community is bound together

> because their fellowship with the machine was deep and strong; stronger than the barriers which separated them from their employers, stronger even than the obstacle which until now had been insurmountable—the colour of their skin. (p. 77)

It is Fa Keita, the elder and sage of Bamako who makes a poignant summary of the new situation:

> 'Long ago . . . before any of you were born, everything that happened happened within a framework, an order that was our own, and the existence of that order was of great importance in our lives. Today no such framework exists. There are no castes among people, no difference in the quality of grain or of the bread that is made from the grain; there are no weavers, no artisans in metal, no makers of fine shoes.
>
> I think it is the machine which has ground everything together this way and brought everything to a single level.' (p. 94)

It is this consciousness of a common destiny which creates in the workers the will to act together and to subordinate their private interests to those of the community.

The actual mechanism by which the workers achieve their objectives is somewhat over-simplified. After a number of scenes in which we are shown the general mood of dissatisfaction among the workers, a strike is set in motion almost by accident. During a single session in which there is a minimum of debate the impatient railway workers decide to go on strike.

After the strike has started the workers have two alternatives: either to hold out until their demands are met or to surrender to the pressure of their exploiters and lose the struggle. The weeks that follow the decision to strike test the endurance of the workers to the full. First there is the idleness of unemployment which is followed by acute poverty and the very serious prospect of starvation as supplies are deliberately cut off by the capitalist masters. Then the frustration of the workers drives them into inevitable physical conflict with their masters. Incidents of violence become frequent and many workers lose their lives in the conflict.

In their hour of trial the workers are always in danger of subverting their unity through recrimination as their hardships accumulate. The strike starts as a voluntary thing but later it becomes necessary to coerce, to judge and even to molest others as some of them lose nerve or become tempted by selfish motives to betray the common cause. As they get involved in the charges and counter-charges of betrayal they fall into the danger of losing sight of the noble ideals of the struggle and becoming involved in petty hatred. But the leaders make them realize that their oppressors have always capitalized on their divisions and are always ready to encourage and even create new divisions as well as magnify the old ones. The fellowship in suffering makes them aware of the need for a common front. The strike becomes the occasion for bringing out the noblest qualities in the community. Old women like Ramatoulaye demonstrate qualities of endurance and initiative which we would never have suspected them to possess. Ndeye Touti, the brainwashed schoolgirl who has been accustomed to looking down upon her community now identifies with her own kind and becomes involved in a physical struggle on their behalf. Even Penda, the licentious and selfish woman, shows qualities of leadership and dedication to the community which make everyone change their mind about her. It is the physical and moral tests that the workers have to endure that bring to the surface the noble qualities of their natures. At the most critical point in the struggle, during the long march to Dakar, Bakayoko learns that his mother is dead, his daughter injured and his father arrested; but he goes forward with the march because he rates the interests of the community higher than those of the family. It is this exemplary and charismatic quality of sacrifice that enables him to inspire the workers at this most critical hour in the struggle. Even the children find an unexpected role when they start shooting birds and lizards to feed their families.

The main protagonist of the novel is the workers' movement. Our identification is with this movement, not with individuals. No individual is allowed to claim our sympathy beyond the occasional moment. Even Bakayoko, the leader, is distanced and in many ways he is more of an ideal than an individual. The incidents and episodes are too numerous to be remembered. So are the characters. This means that we remember the bare outlines of the plot and the characters lose their identity in the railway workers' movement.

Sembene Ousmane experiments with the handling of the sensibilities of crowds and groups of people. The people who take part in the strike remain mere workers and we sympathize with them at the general level. In spite of occasional glimpses we never see them as fathers and mothers, lovers and rivals, believers or cynics. The sympathy which the author accords them is total and the reader has no option. But our identification is with the common cause rather than with individuals. Many of the individuals we never remember and they could as well have remained nameless. The author is not concerned with their private destinies but with the destiny of the workers' movement. Individual persons are insignificant; it is the Railway Union that counts. Ousmane always directs our interest to the collective mass of labourers and their collective bargaining for social benefits. Individuals may jump ahead of the crowd to wave a flag or sometimes to get shot, but they remain part of the crowd. All those who die—and there are numerous deaths in the novel—die accidentally in the crowd and after a moment of pathos we forget about them. We never see who is grieved by these deaths. There is no mourning and no ceremony. The crowd marches on. The importance of these deaths and other forms of suffering which we witness is that they are gestures made on behalf of the community. The workers collectively win recognition for the sanctity of their life as expressed through their labour. They revolt against being treated as mere numbers, or as units of labour. They win their claim to being treated as a valuable collection of 'God's bits of wood'.

The novel is concerned more with what is probable than with what happens in ordinary life. In this respect it is closer to romance than to realism. The characters are more of archetypes than real people. Even Bakayoko, the idealized trade union leader remains an abstract ideal. Our acquaintance with him is mainly through the aphorisms and axioms that he has coined for the workers. It is he who has uttered the words that act as inspiration for many of the workers:

> It isn't those who are taken by force, put in chains and sold as slaves who are the real slaves: it is those who will accept it, morally and physically. (p. 20)

It is aphorisms such as this that give inspiration to the workers' rebellion. But Ousmane deliberately plays down the heroism of the trade union leaders. Although Bakayoko is regarded both by the workers and the colonial bosses as the brain behind the strike his actions are shown to be of little significance. The confrontation with the railway bosses is not planned in detail by any committee. It is the anger and the will of the workers that sustains the rebellion. And the not-so-much-spoken-about organizers such as Lahbib and Duodu perform more decisive roles than the idealized leaders of the movement. But, ultimately, the success of the resistance depends upon the spontaneous anger of the workers. No individual is more important than the masses he leads. All the leaders show themselves at their best when they participate in the same actions as the workers they lead. When Bakayoko joins the march from Thies to Dakar he becomes part of the workers' movement, not its leader. The crowd, as it flows towards Dakar, is compared to an irresistible current which is confidently flowing towards the future. This is the climax and resolution of the novel. The workers who have hitherto been indifferent or hesitant are drawn spontaneously into the march and the traitors are humiliated.

The moral is too pointed to be missed. The masses of Africa should be united in order to defeat the exploiters. In the final march the human mass flows like a river, irresistibly towards the future. The personal sacrifices and the heroism of the workers in their hour of struggle bring about the desirable goal of freedom. This is 'the-novelist-as-teacher' driving home his lesson to the people of Africa.

Although the author refrains from direct comment the use of puppet figures is maximized. This need not necessarily imply criticism, for psychological exploration lies beyond the author's purpose. What often makes the reader uneasy is the presentation of the crowd as if it were an organic entity capable of reacting with uniform feelings and thoughts. Here for example is the description of the sense of loss which the workers of Dakar seem to share equally as a result of the idleness brought about by the strike:

> Like rejected lovers returning to a trysting place, they kept coming back to the areas surrounding the stations. . . . For a few minutes they would wander along the rails and then, suddenly, as though seized with panic, they would hasten back to the safety of the group they had left. Then again they would just stand there, or squat down in the shade of a sand hill, their eyes fixed on the two endless parallels, following them out until they joined and lost themselves in the brush. Something was being born inside them, as if the past and the future were coupling to breed a new kind of man, and it seemed to them that the wind was whispering a phrase they had often heard from Bakayoko: 'The kind of man we were is dead, and our only hope for a new life lies in the machine, which knows neither a language nor a race.' (p. 76)

It is impossible to visualize a crowd watching the same point on the horizon and thinking exactly the same thought. Such presentation of aggregate feeling sometimes prevents us from seeing the personalities in the novel as real people rather than as representatives of social viewpoints.

God's Bits of Wood is Sembene Ousmane's best-known novel. After it he had planned to write 4 novels linked together on the model of Balzac's *Comédie Humaine*. But he has felt that fiction is not reaching the working class people for whom he is writing. He has now turned to film as a more effective way of reaching ordinary people. He thus remains committed to using art for political action.

NOTES

1. Ngugi, *Weep Not, Child*, African Writers Series, Heinemann Educational Books Ltd, London, 1964.
2. Kariuki, Josiah M., *Mau Mau Detainee*, Oxford University Press, London, 1963.
3. Mboya, Tom, *Freedom and After*, André Deutsch, London, 1963.
4. Mazrui, Ali, *On Heroes and Uhuru Worship*, Longmans, London, 1967, p. 21.
5. Ngugi, 'Satire in Nigeria', Pieterse, Cosmo and Munro, Donald (eds.), *Protest and Conflict in African Literature*, Heinemann, London, 1969, p. 69.
6. Wastberg, Per (ed.), *The Writer in Modern Africa*, African-Scandinavian Writers' Conference, Stockholm, Uppsala, 1968, p. 25.
7. Kenyatta, Jomo, *Facing Mount Kenya*, Mercury Books, London, 1961, p. 21.
8. Kariuki, *op. cit.*
9. Balandier, G., 'Messianism and Nationalism in Black Africa', in Berghe, Pierre van der (ed.), *Africa: Problems of Change and Conflict*, Chandler, San Francisco, 1965, p. 443.
10. Elders, Derek, 'A Grain of Wheat', *African Literature Today*, no. 1, London, March 1968.
11. Nazareth, Peter, 'An African Writer and Commitment', *Transition*, vol. 4, no. 19, Kampala, Feb. 1965.

Conclusion: Realism and the African Novel

Three separate but often overlapping traditions can be identified in the development of the modern novel. The first consists of those novels which, through their selection of facts and details from ordinary life, produce the 'illusion of reality' by creating a picture of a world that closely resembles our own. This tradition is normally referred to as realism. The second consists of those novels which, through their projection of idealistic or distorted values create a picture of life that does not correspond to the world that we know, the result being romance or caricature, depending on whether human possibilities are expanded or reduced. The realist mode may be said to express 'scientific truth'. The other mode, often called romance, may be said to express 'poetic truth'. There is yet a third category of novels which, through their fusion of the first two modes, seek to express man's relationship with the universe. This mode is most characteristic of twentieth century *avant garde* literature and the kind of truth it tries to express may be vaguely termed 'metaphysical'.

The three modes are difficult to separate because they often overlap, even in a single work of art, as many modern novelists borrow techniques from all the three traditions of fiction. The distinction is therefore being made in terms of emphasis, an emphasis which enables us to see how the realist mode differs from the other modes of fiction. With the non-realist schools a high premium is accorded to overriding aesthetic principles. In the realist tradition the highest premium goes to accuracy of observation in terms of known facts. This explains why realism is the best instrument for analysing individual behaviour and the social patterns of a given society.

There are two types of realism: the first type concerns itself primarily with the behaviour of man, the individual being treated as an autonomous entity. The second type takes the whole breadth of society as its subject matter and examines how the customs, conventions, social institutions and individuals inter-relate. The first type is what has come to be known as psychological realism, the second as social realism. With social realism, the individual is treated as a social unit; most often he is silhouetted against the institutions, traditions and general behaviour of his society so as to underscore his insignificance. His aspirations, achievements and disappointments are seen as conditioned by his place in a given society and can be used to raise wider ethical, moral and social issues.

Social realism became a major fictional technique in nineteenth century Europe and it may be said to constitute the central inheritence of the African novel from its European ancestor. In essence and technique the African novel has borrowed heavily from the European novel. Compared with poetry and drama the African novel has been shy of experiment. The best African poets have not written odes, elegies and sonnets. They have invented new models to embody their reactions to modern life. The inventiveness of Okot p'Bitek, Soyinka and Okara immediately comes to mind. And in drama Soyinka, Serumaga and J. P. Clark have greatly exploited the folk traditions of their people and arrived at new forms of dramatic expressions. By contrast, the leading African novelists have been satisfied with employing the techniques developed by European realism and have used them to comment upon African experience. Local colour is there—in Achebe, Laye, Ngugi and Oyono—but the basic form remains unaltered.

Social realism should offer a clear and graspable conception of the relationship between individuals and their society. The nineteenth century novel in Europe often shows individuals being oppressed by rigid social norms. This oppression is most acutely felt by sensitive individuals whom we meet as central characters in *Middlemarch*, *Anna Karenina* and *Madame Bovary*, to mention but a few. In these same novels we see how the lives of some characters become reduced as they are turned into mechanical dolls through their uncritical acceptance of the conventions of society. At the same time, other individuals are criticized for their failure to make reasonable adjustments to satisfy the expectations of their society.

In the African novel the only instances where the criticism of society is based on the tyranny of its norms are in the novels of the past, as in *The Concubine*[1] and *Things Fall Apart*. In novels which portray contemporary experience, criticism of society tends to dwell on the very absence of norms which can provide the individual with a basis for good conduct. The individual is often portrayed struggling to set up his own code of conduct and the society mostly failing to appreciate the difficult dilemma of the man of conscience. In rare circumstances the individual may establish an admirable code of conduct in spite of great and discouraging pressures. The hero of *A Wreath for Udomo* is a good example of such a rare achievement. A great many individuals portrayed in African fiction, however, become victims of erroneous choices because society has failed to guide them into rightful conduct. Oyono's *Houseboy* and Beti's *Mission to Kala* are good illustrations of this.

In the social imbroglio which constitutes the contemporary life of Africa certain evil geniuses take advantage of this lack of community will to satisfy their private interests and gratify their animal desires. The most memorable of this type of individual is Chief Nanga of *A Man of the People*. Even here the society is still to be blamed for its failure to impose restraint upon such men. In the long run such men usually destroy themselves through overreaching. Certain other men who are neither evil nor heroic enough to actively oppose the evils they see around them are forced into social withdrawal. Such types are represented in the heroes of *The Beautyful Ones Are Not Yet Born* and *The Gab Boys* as well as in the rebellious group of young men that we meet in Soyinka's *The Interpreters*. The authors tend to have an indulgent attitude towards such characters for their rebelliousness, but the characters are never allowed to rise to the stature of heroes.

All the types that are represented in African fiction face the task of defining their duty towards their community. It is this that determines whether we judge them as good or bad men. There is never any possibility of total rebellion against society because there is no uniform body of norms to rebel against. Society has very ill-defined expectations from its members and this is why so often people cannot distinguish true leaders from false ones. The only norms that are recognizable are those which are set up from time to time by the ruling or privileged classes. It is against such false norms that the man of conscience revolts.

The African novel has attained maturity in a relatively short period of time because it did not have to go through a long evolutionary process. The reasons why the novel emerged in Africa as a dominant form when it did lie outside the scope of this book. However, we may observe in passing that by the middle of the twentieth century there existed in Africa certain social factors that had wide correspondences with those which gave birth to the novel in eighteenth-century Europe. Increased literacy, the increased leisure that goes with urbanization, the growth of a commercial middle class and the dominance of science over magic and superstition are some of the major factors.

But our main interest here is in answering the question why the novel has become the principal literacy vehicle for analysing and commenting upon contemporary life in Africa. The answer lies in the very character of the form and the advantages it has over other forms. More than any other form, the novel can evoke the whole way of life of a people at a given time. Through this, or through a selection of interrelated aspects of life, it can analyse the basic social structure of a given society and show how the total life of the individual is affected by the conditions in which he lives. The reader is then able to evaluate these conditions of life by the way they affect individuals. This capacity which the novel alone possesses has been seized upon by African artists and been used to raise issues which go even beyond private conduct into problems of morality in public affairs. Social realism has been the principal tool by which this has been done.

The general tone of the novel is one of restlessness. The society depicted in African fiction shows a people caught up at a cultural cross-roads. Neither the bewildered masses nor the alienated élite are shown to be capable of answering the challenges of their time. These are the conditions which have led to the flourishing of mediocrity in leadership and which sometimes lead the society into making sporadic handshakes with anarchy.

The relative insignificance of the individual is continually emphasized. All the angry young men that we meet in the novels—mostly expectant, naive and idealistic—are made to grapple with the problems of a modern, complex social set-up. Often they are unnerved by its immensity. Sometimes they turn into cynics, sometimes they attain laudable goals; but we always recognize their insignificance, because their very attitudes are conditioned by their decaying environment.

The African novel has developed as a response to the far-reaching social revolution of the twentieth century on the continent. The novelists that have been discussed in the foregoing chapters are those who have tried to come to terms, through their art, with the effects of this revolution that has brought about a complete overhaul of traditional ways of living. This overhaul has extended to ethnic groupings, social structure, agriculture, industry, politics, education, communication and entertainment. In the new complex maze of institutions and values the novelists have tried to search for the basis of a sense of community which is necessary before individuals can feel able to go about the business of life with a sense of certainty.

The values which are asserted by the novelists are those of a detribalized anti-colonial class. It is in this sense that we can see these novels as embodiments of a rebellion, a rebellion against the authoritarian hierarchy of traditional society, the exploitative colonial set-up, the commercialism of the West and the philistine society of post-independence. The novelists, in their different ways, have shown the complex and painful adjustments that individuals have been called upon to make in response to the great changes which their society has rapidly undergone and is still undergoing. Through the specific evocation of particular communities the novelists have been able to express their view of the significance of these changes in the wider context of the basic and more permanent needs and aspirations of man.

The novels which we have discussed may be said to constitute the mainstream of African fiction. This mainstream is informed by a high-minded social awareness. It is fed by novels which, in a serious manner, seek to increase and influence our awareness of the major issues of our time. These novels provide a qualitative evaluation of modern African life. The novelists view themselves primarily as social critics rather than entertainers. But even if we judge a novel as a social document we have to recognize that the writer has to bend to the dictates of artistic propriety before he can make his statement effectively. Therefore, while paying close attention to the kind of criticism each writer has to offer to his society we have avoided treating the novels as social treatises and insisted on viewing them as works of art. The general picture that emerges from this body of criticism of African society is one of Africa as an unweeded garden. The very act of writing fiction has been, for each novelist, a contribution towards the weeding of this garden.

NOTE

1. Amadi, Elechi, *The Concubine*, African Writers Series, Heinemann Educational Books Ltd, London, 1966.

Bibliography of Literary and Social Criticism

Abraham, Willie, *The Mind of Africa*, Weidenfeld & Nicolson, London, 1962.

Achebe, Chinua, *Morning Yet on Creation Day*, Heinemann, London, 1975.

Blyden, Edward, *Christianity, Islam and the Negro Race* (edited by Christopher Fife), Edinburgh University Press, Edinburgh, 1967.

Brench, A. C., *The Novelists' Inheritance in Black Africa*, Oxford University Press, London, 1967.

Cartey, Wilfred, *Whispers from a Continent*, Heinemann, London, 1971.

Duerden, D. and Pierterse, C. (eds), *African Writers Talking*, Heinemann, London, 1972.

Gleason, Judith, *This Africa: Novels by West Africans in English and French*, North Western University Press, Evanston, 1965.

Gurr, Andrew and Zirimu, Pio, *Black Aesthetics*, East African Literature Bureau, Nairobi, 1973.

Howe, Irving, *Politics and the Novel*, Horizon Press, New York, 1967.

Heywood, C., *Perspectives on African Literature*, Heinemann, London, 1971.

Jahn, Janheinz, *A History of Neo-African Literature*, Faber, London, 1968.

Jahn, Janheinz, *A Bibliography of Neo-African Literature*, André Deutsch, London, 1965.

Jones, Eldred (ed), *African Literature Today, No. 5: The Novel in Africa*, Heinemann, London, 1971.

July, Robert, *The Origins of Modern African Thought*, Faber, London, 1968.

Kesteloot, Lilyan, *Les Ecrivains Noirs de Language Française*, Université Libre de Bruxelles, Institut de Sociologie, Brussels, 1965.

Killam, G. D., *African Writers on African Writing*, Heinemann, London, 1972.

——, *The Novels of Chinua Achebe*, Heinemann, London, 1969.

Laurence, Margaret, *Long Drums and Cannons*, Macmillan, London, 1968.

Legum, Colin, *Pan-Africanism*, Pall Mall Press, London, 1965.

Le Vine, Victor, *Political Leadership in Africa*, Stanford University Press, Stanford, 1967.

Lloyd, P. C., *Africa in Social Change: West African Societies in Transition*, Penguin African Library, London, 1967.

Lo Liyong, Taban, *The Last Word*, East African Publishing House, Nairobi, 1969.

Mazrui, A. and Rotberg, R. (eds), *Protest and Power in Black Africa*, Harvard University Centre for International Affairs, New York, 1970.

Moore, Gerald, *Seven African Writers*, Oxford University Press, London, 1962.

——, (ed), *African Literature and the Universities*, Ibadan University Press, Ibadan, 1962.

Mphahlele, Ezekiel, *The African Image*, Faber & Faber, London, 1962.

Nazareth, Peter, *Literature and Society in Modern Africa*, East African Literature Bureau, Nairobi, 1973.

Ngugi wa Thiong'o, *Homecoming*, Heinemann, London, 1972.

Palmer, Eustace, *An Introduction to the African Novel*, Heinemann, London, 1972.

Pieterse, C. and Munro, D. (eds), *Protest and Conflict in African Literature*, Heinemann, London, 1969.

Roscoe, Adrian, *Mother is Gold, A Study in West African Literature*, Heinemann, London, 1969.

Tucker, Martin, *Africa in Modern Literature: A Survey of Contemporary Writing in English*, F. Ungar Pub. Co., New York, 1967.

Van der Berghe, Pierre (ed), *Africa: Problems of Change and Conflict*, Chandler Publishing Co., San Francisco, 1965.

Wallerstein, Emmanuel, *Africa, the Politics of Independence; An Interpretation of Modern African History*, Vintage Books, New York, 1961.

Wanjala, Chris (ed) *Standpoints on African Literature*, East African Literature Bureau, Nairobi, 1973.

Wastberg, Per (ed), *The Writer in Modern Africa*, Almquist and Wiksell, Uppsala, 1967.

Wauthier, Claude, *The Literature and Thought of Modern Africa*, Pall Mall Press, London, 1966.

Wright, Edgar (ed), *The Critical Evaluation of African Literature*, Heinemann, London, 1973.

Index